When Time Warps

When Time Warps

The Lived Experience of Gender, Race, and Sexual Violence

Megan Burke

 University of Minnesota Press
Minneapolis
London

A different version of chapter 1 was published as "Gender as Lived Time: Reading *The Second Sex* for a Feminist Phenomenology of Temporality," *Hypatia: A Journal of Feminist Philosophy* 33, no. 1 (2018): 111–26. A different version of chapter 5 was published as "Specters of Violence," *APA Newsletter on Feminism and Philosophy* 14, no. 2 (2015): 10–18.

Published by the University of Minnesota Press
111 Third Avenue South, Suite 290
Minneapolis, MN 55401-2520
http://www.upress.umn.edu

Printed on acid-free paper

The University of Minnesota is an equal-opportunity educator and employer.

Library of Congress Cataloging-in-Publication Data
Names: Burke, Megan, author.
Title: When time warps : the lived experience of gender, race, and sexual violence / Megan Burke.
Description: Minneapolis : University of Minnesota Press, 2019. | Includes bibliographical references and index.
Identifiers: LCCN 2018061112 (print) | ISBN 978-1-5179-0545-3 (hc) | ISBN 978-1-5179-0546-0 (pb)
Subjects: LCSH: Rape. | Sex crimes. | Patriarchy.
Classification: LCC HV6558 .B875 2019 (print) | DDC 364.15/32—dc23
LC record available at https://lccn.loc.gov/2018061112

UMP KEP

To those who have encouraged my feminist perception

Contents

"You Rape Our Women"

Rethinking Gender, Race, and Rape

On June 17, 2015, Dylan Storm Roof entered the Emanuel African Methodist Episcopal Church in Charleston, South Carolina, and opened fire on African American congregants attending a Bible study. Roof murdered nine people with a .45 caliber pistol he purchased with birthday money. A self-declared white supremacist, Roof announced his reason for the massacre to the all-black congregation: "You rape our women, and you're taking over our country" (Workman and Kannapell 2015).[1] Once under police custody, Roof reiterated this justification for the hate crime: "I had to do it because somebody had to do something because black people are killing white people every day on the street and they rape, they rape white women, 100 white women a day" (U.S. Attorney's Office 2015).[2]

In the context of U.S. history, Roof's white supremacist terrorism is neither exceptional nor an isolated event. White Americans, whether self-declared white supremacists or not, have a long history of massacres against communities and people of color. Yet in the wake of Roof's white terrorism, America became obsessed with isolating the white supremacist motive of his act. Although the American public was informed that Roof without a doubt is a white supremacist—and indeed this is undeniable since he said so himself—there was a fetishistic interest in Roof as self-radicalized. Indeed, the majority of inquiries into the motive of white supremacy individualize Roof's hate, taking his white supremacy as the effect of an individual white boy gone awry because of his access to radical literature on the Internet. The mainstream American public even learned, in a typical white response to white supremacy, that Roof had black friends, as if to insist that Roof must be a pathological individual who radicalized himself rather than the embodiment of a contemporary white supremacist—someone who can simultaneously have black friends and massacre black people.[3]

To the majority of readers of this book, the effort to package Roof's white supremacy as individual and pathological for the mainstream (white) American public should not be surprising. Given the enduring and systemic failure of white Americans to deal with the sociohistorical reality that white supremacist terror is a national pastime, the popular response to Roof is anything but extraordinary. The majority of the media coverage of Roof was structured by the entrenched white American neglect of recognizing white supremacist violence as a historical and ordinary venture of white men, even the ones with black friends. What interests me here is a more nuanced feminist examination of Roof's justification for his white supremacist terrorism and its neglect in the dominant American social imaginary. From an intersectional feminist perspective, Roof's rationale is one that is racialized, sexualized, and gendered. He draws on the historical legacy of the myth of the black male rapist and the symbolic nationalist image of white female vulnerability as legitimate realities of the present. His testimonies make visible the way the historical past is profoundly present. Thinking as a feminist would in relation to Roof—paying attention to the way a racialized heterogendered system structures and becomes a justification for action—discloses that our contemporary gender schemas are profoundly entangled in old white supremacist myths of rape and commitments to disempowered white womanhood.

Although it might be tempting and comforting to think that only a radical minority of white individuals like Roof hold on to violent gender ideology and the historical images of the lecherous black man and the pure, vulnerable white woman, these controlling images have not been left in the past.[4] Rather, Roof is explicit testimony to the way historical constructs and processes of heterosexist racism are deeply encrusted in and profoundly structure the living present of gender and race—a present that is often bound to violence or its threat. A consideration of the racialized and sexualized gender narratives at work in Roof's testimonies means grappling with the intransigence of the dominant gender schema in the United States. It requires confronting the endurance of racist conceptions and uses of rape as the justification for and institution of gender ideology and white supremacy. It is to face a very material haunting of the past. From a feminist perspective, what is striking about Roof's testimonies is not merely that they draw on heteropatriarchy and white supremacy (that is quite ordinary) but that in doing so, some very traditional racialized gender commitments are exposed. If, rather than individualizing and pathologizing Roof's white supremacy one takes seriously Roof as one manifestation of a larger racialized gender apparatus, then the disclosure of allegedly antiquated gender ideology is not isolated. To me, what is important and horrifying about wrestling with Roof's actions and justification is that it demands an account of the way white supremacist heterosexist domination remains at the heart of a nation and lived experience.

A number of women of color feminists have pointed out that such domination is constitutive of a persistent racialized gender hierarchy (hooks 1981; Davis 1981; Lugones 2007). Building on such work, in this book I account for how such racialized sexual domination and corresponding ideologies, exemplified by but in no way limited to Roof, are disclosed in the contemporary lived experience of gender. This phenomenological reckoning turns, however, not to the white masculine subject represented by Roof but to the way white ideologies about rape like the ones deployed by Roof are pervasive in and structure women's existence. Many feminist scholars have talked at length about the relation between gender and space and the spatial landscape or geography of the fear of rape (Young 1980; Valentine 1989; Cahill 2001; Hollander 2001). Feminist phenomenologists in particular have accounted for how women's existence is spatially constituted as a normatively feminine one—an inhibited, confined, and constrained subjectivity—in tacit and ordinary ways through the fear of rape, sexual violence, and heterosexist domination (Young 1980; Bartky 1990; Cahill 2001; Vera-Grey 2017). Building on and departing from this work, I consider how women's embodied existence is realized through particular relations to and experiences of time that are structured in large part by racist and heterosexist tropes, ideologies, realities, and histories of sexual violence. In this book, I refer to this constellation of practices as sexual domination. My particular aim is to develop a feminist phenomenology of the temporality of feminine subjectivity that discloses how racialized colonial sexual domination is temporally woven into the fabric of that subjectivity. This turn to temporality reveals in a different way than considerations of space do the constitutive weight of sexual domination in women's lived experience. It also underscores the centrality of sexualized racism in the production of feminine existence and shows that temporalities of domination and trauma mark one as a woman.

In the context of this inquiry, feminine existence is not equivalent to femininity as a particular gender presentation or expression. One can be feminine or perform or do femininity in ways unrelated and even in resistance to a feminine existence. Feminine existence refers to a constrained mode of gendered embodiment through which one becomes a woman that is often realized over the course of life events, but it can also be a temporary experience. As a conceptual term, it emerges from Simone de Beauvoir's ([1949] 2010) description of a particular way in which human beings in a sexist society become women by taking up or assuming bodily habits and social practices that render one a sexualized passivity—being made and making oneself a passive existence for men. Although these habits and social practices may be taken to be an expression of femininity, on a Beauvoirian account it is not so much how one looks, what clothes one wears, what one's interests are, whether one is more or less emotional, and so forth that matters. Rather, the main issue is one's relation to freedom. A feminine existence is a gendered existence that lives freedom through men and thus lives a relative existence. A feminine existence is not necessarily synonymous with "woman" as a gender identity or subjectivity, but insofar as it is a mode of existence that confers recognition in a heteromasculinist world, many girls and women embark on realizing a feminine existence even if, at some points, they rebel and protest. At the same time, even if one does not make oneself a woman in this way or does not make oneself a woman at all, one can assume a feminine existence by being rendered in this way by others. One can, for instance, be taken as a woman who exists for men and is treated accordingly even if one does not understand oneself to be a woman. That is, one's gendered existence can be misread or misgendered in ways that hurl them into a feminine existence. One can also be taken as a feminine existence but in some way fail to comply and thus be violently hurled into another abject position. Or a person who comfortably assumes existence as a woman might go to great lengths to resist normative feminine habits but nevertheless embodies them when harassed on the street.

From a phenomenological view, then, feminine existence refers to a particular way of assuming one's concrete situation in relation to freedom. This feminist phenomenology considers how this relation is assumed through temporal legacies and structures of racialized heterosexist domination. But insofar as one's lived experience or social positioning as a woman is constituted through a complex field of social structures and classificatory schemas, who can assume a feminine existence, whom it is imposed on, and who is interpellated through its ideological framework is profoundly dependent on one's assigned gender, sexuality, race, class, and national status as well as one's geopolitical location. Indeed, feminine existence is often reserved for those who are or are taken to be white, cisgender, middle-class, heterosexual women and constituted through and against physical, sexual, or ontological violence of women of other social locations that have historically barred them from the material and social privileges of white, cis, heteronormative femininity.

Although I draw attention to the way sexual domination is anchored into feminine existence through temporality, I do not wish to minimize the prevalence of gender-based violence and sexual domination in the lives of other marginalized groups.[5] While it is certainly the case that white, cisgender, middle-class women experience rape at high rates and that cisgender women in sexist and misogynist contexts are subject to heterosexist domination, rates of rape among noncis, nonhetero, nonwhite, non-Western, and poor populations are most likely even higher, and their experiences of oppression on the basis of norms of gender and sexuality are not only just as pervasive but are also structured and experienced in different, often more brutal ways. Even though I do not detail these lived experiences of violence and domination, my account is motivated by the connection between the relation of the production and maintenance of a system of normative gender to violence against those who cannot or do not inhabit it (Butler [1990] 1999, 1993; Bettcher 2006, 2007). Thus, my account of the temporality of feminine existence considers how temporality, the lived experience of time, not only reveals the centrality of sexual domination in women's lives but also discloses a tacit embodied operation of normative gender (white, cis, hetero) in subjective life, which in turn reifies violence— physical, sexual, social, and ontological—against other marginalized populations. Whereas queer theorists have largely focused on the way reproductive temporalities normatively configure gendered subjects and exile queer bodies, I draw attention to the way the normative gendered subjectivity of feminine existence is constituted as temporality, a disclosure of ideological and historical constructions of racism and heterosexism at the level of the lived experience of time.

My choice to give an account of feminine existence is an effort to consider how, in spite of certain shifts in cultural patterns and individual habits in the United States that allow those who become girls and women to live and do their gender in ways that have been previously inaccessible, unacceptable, or impossible, such gendered subjects still live a tenuous relation to freedom and how the maintenance of this feeble relation to a future of possibility is a central way racist and heterosexist sexual domination remains woven into gendered existence today. I do, however, think my analysis extends beyond the borders of the geopolitical space of the United States, particularly insofar as American ideologies and institutions circulate through global capitalism and imperialism, and, as I discuss later, insofar as I understand gender to be a colonial institution. However, I do not wish to make any claims as to how it does so and to what extent. I am thinking from multiple concrete places in the United States where I have worked on this project, and although I acknowledge that this limits my account, even in ways I am unaware of, it also electrifies a particular relation between gender, race, temporality, and ideologies and realities of sexual violence. I take it that there are generalizable aspects of my account that will encourage other considerations of gendered existence and temporality, but that is work for others to do.

Feminist Phenomenology

In this book, I take up a critical feminist phenomenological method. This methodological choice means on the one hand that I follow phenomenology as a method that accounts for the temporal structure of human experience, and on the other that I depart from classical commitments that bracket the contingencies of experience, like gender, in order to account for the temporal structure of transcendental consciousness or pure subjectivity.[6] Following previous work by feminist phenomenologists, the feminist phenomenological method I deploy here is steeped in the veritable mess of social life, sifting through rather than below the concrete and contingent domain of embodied experience.

I begin, as feminist phenomenologists long have, from Simone de Beauvoir's *The Second Sex*, arguably the founding text of feminist phenomenology (Simms and Stawarska 2014). Beauvoir's phenomenological reckoning with the woman question appropriates and pushes back against classical phenomenology in unique ways. Beauvoir pays careful attention to the entangled relation between general conditions of human existence—vulnerability, bodily existence, ambiguity, relation to time and space, our need for recognition—and the socially constituted dimension of gender. She thinks from within, rather than above, her concrete situation, and she emphasizes the investigation of everyday embodied experience as a way to account for the meaning of gendered existence (Mann 2014). Beauvoir's phenomenological account of becoming a woman draws on the phenomenological notion of the living body as a way to address the relation between facticity and freedom—that we have bodies with certain functions, physical traits, feelings, and needs, at the same time that we always live our bodies in specific contexts—or, to use Beauvoirian language, total concrete situations. Following Beauvoir, then, throughout this book I use the term "living body" to not only talk about the way social and historical constructs mediate and are taken up in embodied existence but also to underscore that norms of gender are not merely constructed but are first and foremost lived, and indeed undertaken as bodily projects.

On my reading, what is particularly compelling about *The Second Sex* as a phenomenology of feminine existence is that Beauvoir offers a meticulous description of the harm endured when one becomes a woman through heteronormative systems of meaning and cultural practices, which is disclosed in and constituted at and through the juncture of nature and culture—that is, the living body. Following the phenomenological notion of the living (or lived) body, feminist phenomenologists prioritize the notion of lived gender as a way to address the phenomenon of gender without taking up the nature/culture, biological/social, or sex/gender distinctions (Moi 2001; Young 2005; Mann 2014). To consider lived gender is to prioritize that gender is first disclosed in embodied experience. My own phenomenology draws on and develops the theme of temporality in *The Second Sex* as a way to consider the normative structuring and effects of feminine existence as it is lived and embodied.

However, I draw on Beauvoir in the way she draws on classical phenomenology—not as a dutiful daughter but as a methodological resource for examining the concrete ways that historical and material realities of sexual domination are dialed into embodied existence. When helpful, I turn away from Beauvoir and to other phenomenologists like Maurice Merleau-Ponty, as well as to other modes of inquiry, even ones often taken to be starkly incompatible with phenomenology. Moreover, I draw on the insights of women of color philosophers like Angela Davis (1981) and María Lugones (2007); interdisciplinary feminist scholarship on sexual assault, rape, and trauma; and queer theoretical accounts of the temporal production of normative gender in order to anchor my account in a concrete sociopolitical landscape and to take seriously the insights about the lived experience of gender that are overlooked or underdeveloped by Beauvoir and otherwise absent from the tradition of phenomenology. So although this inquiry is indebted to certain phenomenological descriptions and concepts and their uses within phenomenology, I am not trying to fit the phenomena of concern here into the conceptual frameworks of phenomenology. Insofar as gender is profoundly personal and visceral, but also political and structural, and always at the intersection of other social positions—that is, inasmuch as gender works through and in various ways—the phenomenological method of this book opens itself to ways of thinking that are often taken to be at odds with phenomenology.

When necessary, I address the tensions between the phenomenological tradition and the other modes of inquiry I use. My goal is not to resolve these tensions but to suggest that thinking in different ways might be the best way to do a feminist phenomenology. I have sought to develop a feminist phenomenology of gender and temporality shaped in part by Beauvoir because I find Beauvoir's description of the embodied experience and justificatory structure of feminine existence to be invaluable to a feminist account of the operation of normative gender formation. And although whether doing feminist phenomenology or doing it in the way I am is actually postphenomenological might be a question that arises, it is not one that will be addressed in this book (Oksala 2006).

Key Concepts: Temporality and Sexual Domination

In an effort to denaturalize and contextualize the concrete production of gender, feminist scholarship has predominantly drawn attention to the temporal character of gender in two ways: as historical construct and social repetition. These considerations and theoretical frameworks for thinking gender are invaluable with regard to an analysis of gender as constructed and realized over a course of personal and historical events in a given social context. They demand an engagement with the various ways gender is enmeshed in a complex web of social and historical processes and events. However, they do not capture how particular structures of time constitute gendered subjectivities, how gendered subjects live time, or how the temporal existence of gendered subjects is changed through particular experiences.[7] I rely on a phenomenological notion of temporality to address these questions without, however, dismissing the historical and socially constituted character of gender.

For the phenomenologist, there is a difference between ordinary clock time and temporality—the experience of time or time as it is lived. As such, a phenomenology of temporality accounts for the temporal conditions of human existence and articulates how time shows itself in the life of the subject. Although classical and existential phenomenologists like Martin Heidegger, Edmund Husserl, Emmanuel Levinas, and Merleau-Ponty are traditionally engaged in phenomenological considerations of temporality, I appeal to Beauvoir's discussions of temporality in *The Second Sex* in order to develop a feminist phenomenology of temporality that reveals that experiences of time are never separate from gender, at least in contexts in which gender is a central feature of subjective life. Indeed, as I will argue later on, a feminist phenomenology underscores the co-constitutive relationship between the contingent phenomenon of gender and the tripartite structure of temporality as a general structure of human existence. In doing so, I draw on the phenomenological tradition's claim that every subjective experience has a triadic temporal structure—a relation to the past, present, and future—but I suggest that to live a feminine existence is to inhabit a particular relation to the past, present, and future.[8] Accordingly, this entire book is a meditation on what kind of experience of time this is, how it takes shape, how it affects existence, and what its social and political effects are. When appropriate, I also use the insights of classical and existential phenomenology to guide various aspects of my inquiry and to further develop a feminist phenomenology. My appeal to Beauvoir's discussion of temporality is also motivated by her account of the way heterosexist domination structures the temporal existence of a woman and how experiences of sexual domination change the way one lives time. In my view, a Beauvoirian explanation of the relation between temporality and feminine existence captures something important about the way sexual domination can materialize in its most extreme form as rape and also in ordinary ways as an experience of time.

My account is not, then, about acts of sexual violence or the experience of surviving a sexual assault or rape. I am interested in the ways ideologies and historical realities of sexual violence structure and are central to the lived reality of feminine existence in particular. I understand the presence of such ideologies and realities as a particular mode of sexual domination. Sexual domination, although rarely explicitly defined, has long been a central theme in feminist scholarship on rape and heterosexism. In a feminist context, rape is taken to be a gendered crime; a particular expression of gendered power through violence, abuse, or force that is sexual;[9] and a key instrument in the creation and maintenance of interlocking systems of domination. Although feminist scholars account for rape in numerous, often conflicting ways, there is nevertheless a central commitment to an account of the harm of rape as sexual domination—that is, as a denial of agency and personhood achieved through a particular gendered use of sex. Because of the persistent prevalence of rape against women by men, "rape is, for many feminists," Ann Cahill writes, "the ultimate expression of a patriarchal order, a crime that epitomizes women's oppressed status by proclaiming, in the loudest voice possible, the most degrading truths about women that a hostile world has to offer" (2001, 2). However, feminists also draw attention to other pernicious and tacit expressions of sexual domination. These discussions highlight how heteromasculinist economies of desire, heterosexist sexual objectification, and the threat of rape are pervasive denials of agency and subjectivity, making a woman, as Cahill claims, "a pre-victim" (2001, 160). These expressions of sexual domination are taken to be produced by and support a rape culture—that is, a historical and social environment in which rape is normalized. A rape culture is, however, much more than the normalization of rape. It is also the emergence and institutionalization of a constellation of historical processes as well as social and interpersonal relations and practices of sexual domination as an effect of the normalization of rape and as that which reifies it.

From this view, as a concept in and a conceptual framework central to this book, sexual domination should not be considered as equivalent to dominance feminism, which offers a particular account of women's subordination as a result of men's systemic sexualized control over women, or with conceptions and practices of sexual domination as they emerge in ethical bondage, discipline, dominance, submissive, sadistic, or masochistic sexual practices. Instead, my use of the phrase "sexual domination" refers to a collection of various uses of sex and sexualized control, which might include rape, the threat of rape, or sexual ideologies that structure interpersonal and social relations in harmful ways, to assert power over and render women inferior as women in relation to men. I acknowledge that rape is a distinct and brutal materialization of sexual domination, and I also acknowledge that there are other forms of it. As much feminist scholarship shows, sexual domination of women by men, in its various forms, is a central weapon of white supremacist heteropatriarchy insofar as it systematically undermines women's agency and denies them freedom.

My consideration of the pervasive yet tacit ideologies and legacies of sexual violence asks how feminine existence is denied an experience of time as a dynamic and open gestalt. In some ways, feminist scholars of trauma have begun to offer such an account. They elucidate the way an experience of rape in particular changes one's relation to time. According to feminist psychiatrist Judith Herman, trauma entails a "rupture in continuity between present and past" that shatters the selfhood of the survivor—a shattering that is maintained when a survivor dissociates from her present (1992, 89). Susan Brison's philosophical meditation on her own experience of the trauma of rape underscores the temporality of trauma's self-shattering. For Brison, "shattered assumptions about the world and one's place in it" leaves the survivor empty and alone in the world (2003, 50). This experience of being alone is constituted by a temporal interruption, a wound that severs one's relation to the past and future, resulting in a disintegration of the self. The survivor, so drastically transformed through the experience of rape, can no longer make sense of who she was and where she was going, and as a result is deserted in the present moment. Or, to follow feminist trauma psychiatrist Bonnie Burstow, survivors of the trauma of rape "tend to become frozen in time" (2003, 1303). At various points in this project, I draw on these accounts to think about the temporal structure of an experience of sexual domination; however, it is not my intention to give a phenomenology of the temporality of rape. Instead, I focus on the temporal experience of the previctim—that is, of feminine existence—which, as I will show, has much in common with that of a survivor of rape. This parallel opens up questions about rape culture as a trauma culture and normative gender subjectivity as a form of trauma.

Throughout this project I consider the way sexual domination operates as a gender constraint through temporality. It is not my intention to suggest that the lived experience of gender has not changed or is inflexible. I am suggesting, however, that it is certainly not inchoate. In this book, I take seriously how collective and individual pasts constitute how gender and time are lived as an embodied inheritance of and in the service of racialized sexual domination.

A Matter of Time

This book is organized into four parts: the prologue, the past, the present, and the future.

The prologue lays the conceptual ground for the inquiry. In chapter 1, I read Beauvoir's *The Second Sex* as a feminist phenomenology of temporality. This reading shifts the dominant Anglo-American reading of Beauvoir's notion of becoming to an account of becoming a woman as a temporality. I argue that a central but unthematized aspect of Beauvoir's work is that it shows how, in sexist and misogynist milieus, one becomes a woman through a particular relation to and lived experience of time: the passive present. This temporality is a central way sexual domination is encrusted into feminine existence.

Part I situates the inquiry in the concrete past in order to show how the historical past structures the present schema and lived experience of gender, especially feminine existence. This section looks at how three historical phenomena—the colonial construction of gender, the colonial use of rape, and the white supremacist myth of the nonwhite male rapist—configure contemporary gendered experience. By tracing the historical past into the present, I offer a critical analysis of the role of white ideologies, myths, and uses of gender and rape in the construction and experience of gender and race. In chapter 2, I build on the work of María Lugones to develop an account of how a colonial temporal structure is keyed into colonial genders. Drawing on Lugones's conceptual framework of the colonial/modern gender system in particular, this chapter underscores the way the notion of gender is the result of colonial linearity that is created and maintained through racialized deployments of rape. Moreover, this chapter considers what it means to inherit gender as a colonial category in lived experience and how that inheritance takes shape through the rape of women of color. Chapter 3 extends the discussion of the constitutive relation between gender, colonial processes, and rape through a consideration of the legacy of the myth of the black male rapist. Beginning with a more recent disclosure of the myth, namely President Donald Trump's use of the myth to criminalize Mexican and Mexican American men in the 2016 presidential race, I reflect on its significance as a regulatory gender apparatus in American life. However, I do so by turning to another rape myth: the myth of stranger rape. I link this historical deployment of the myth of the black male rapist to the popular belief in the myth of stranger rape or the real rape script and argue that they are the same myth. This allows me to situate the myth in relation to phenomenological discussions of the fear/threat of rape in order to develop an intersectional analysis of how the historical constructs of sexualized racism actualize the temporality of feminine existence in girls' and women's lives today and sustain a colonial gender system.

Part II considers how the past is lived in the present in order to highlight the way the presence of gender, especially as it is realized and experienced through historical legacies of sexual domination, is often lived as an absence. Central to this section is a rapprochement between feminist poststructuralism and feminist phenomenology. In chapter 4, I reevaluate Judith Butler's conception of gender subjectivity as a temporal phenomenon, particularly as a performative repetition, through a reading of Merleau-Ponty's notion of anonymous temporality. Merleau-Ponty's discussion of the anonymous character of subjectivity allows for a consideration of gender that underscores its habitual character in a way that prioritizes embodied temporality as central to, but not the cause of, the actualization of gender subjectivity. Moreover, his account also offers a way to address how feminine existence is constituted through an embodied forgetting, which underscores the ontological heaviness and thus intransigence of normative gender in subjective life. Chapter 5 returns to an explicit address of the centrality of sexual domination in the actualization of feminine existence through the notion of spectral violence. Through a reading of Butler's notion of the specters of the abject and Jacques Derrida's notion of hauntology, I draw attention to one experience of sexual domination—the fear of rape—as a constitutive haunting in women's everyday experience. As such, following Butler, I argue that the specter of rape acts as a constitutive temporal constraint. I extend this account of the temporal constraint of the fear of rape to scholarship on rape and the trauma of rape, including, among others, the work of Herman and Brison, and draw a connection between the temporal structure of an experience of rape and the existential ramifications and production of feminine subjectivity in a rape culture. I conclude with the suggestion of a feminist political practice of ghostbusting as a way to address and stage resistance to the existential effect of specters.

Part III concludes by turning to the question of freedom. Whereas the beginning and middle of the book are an effort to take seriously the longer and thicker temporal processes that shape feminine existence, the book's final temporal turn is toward the future. In chapter 6, I draw attention to the affective character of temporality, arguing that a feminist politics of temporality is necessary to the disruption of the legacies and actualization of racialized gender and sexual domination. Drawing on feminist readings of Henri Bergson, Lisa Guenther's critical phenomenology of doing time, and queer theory, I offer an account of three modes of temporal disruption that aim to reconfigure the structure and experience of gender and temporality in order to show how our experiences of time matter in the pursuit and gendered embodiment of freedom.

Prologue

The structure of the present is grounded in temporality. Every human problem cries out to be considered on the basis of time, the ideal being that the present always serves to build the future.

—Frantz Fanon, *Black Skin, White Masks*

1

Toward a Feminist Phenomenology of Temporality and Feminine Existence

> Becoming a woman is breaking with the past, without recourse; but this
> particular passage is more dramatic than any other; it creates a hiatus
> between yesterday and tomorrow; it tears the young girl from the
> imaginary world where a great part of her existence took place and hurls
> her into the real world.
>
> —Simone de Beauvoir, *The Second Sex*

Simone de Beauvoir's rich description of becoming a woman offers a detailed account of the way girls and women are encouraged to make themselves passive, particularly in and through sexualized relations with men,
in order to realize themselves as women—that is, to become women in a
misogynist world. Beauvoir suggests that becoming a woman, becoming
a passivity, is a developmental achievement, a "vocation . . . imperiously
breathed into her from the first years of her life" (2010, 283). She details at
almost dizzying lengths how the social and embodied destiny of womanhood entails learning to experience one's body as a passive thing, to perceive and feel oneself as a doll, and to experience the world as a closure.
The little girl who is thrown into the world as a not yet but potential
woman, learns that the "sphere she belongs to is closed everywhere, limited, dominated by the male universe: as high as she climbs, as far as she
dares go, there will always be a ceiling over her head, walls that block her
path. . . . Because she is woman, the girl knows that the sea and the poles,
a thousand adventures, a thousand joys, are forbidden to her: she is born
on the wrong side" (311).

To be born on the wrong side, as the little girl is, means that she is
disadvantaged from the get-go. Situated as a woman-to-be, the destiny of
the little girl is to make her self a feminine existence. The consequences
of such self-making, Beauvoir insists, are dire. To become a woman in
this way, one must renounce her self as transcendence, as a freedom, and

become a relative existence, a subject who lives the realm of freedom through the eyes, ears, arms, minds, and mouths of men. For Beauvoir, such abdication is fundamentally temporal. As a woman, one is faced with a future that is constituted by men. This impoverished relation to the future mires a woman in a dull and lifeless present. As such, a woman is steeped in immanence, the realm of facticity that makes a woman responsible only for the maintenance of a world she did not create. Barred from realizing herself as freedom, a woman steeps in a frustrated temporal mode in which she awaits the justification of her existence. Beauvoir takes this waiting to be the crucial temporality of feminine existence: "In one sense, her whole existence is a waiting" (649).

In this chapter, my task is to consider what it means to understand a woman as a particular kind of temporality in the way Beauvoir does—that is, as a waiting. What does this suggest about gender? What does this suggest about becoming a woman? By addressing such questions, I give an account of gender as lived time, arguing that temporality is an underlying and thus generative structure of gender. Furthermore, I develop Beauvoir's account of the temporality of becoming a woman in order to show how sexual domination is temporally dialed into feminine existence.

Importantly, it is necessary to point out that Beauvoir's account of becoming a woman is a description that neglects and thus obscures the way processes of racialization—processes structured by local, national, and global racialized political economies—are central to the lived experience of feminine existence. Although Beauvoir had perceived deep structures and experiences of racism in some of her other works, in The Second Sex, she, as Janine Jones puts it, "neglected to say what she had seen in her radical theory of the Other" (2013, 59). As others have noted (Spelman 1988; Simons 1999), Beauvoir's silence on the way race and white supremacy are themselves bound to feminine existence is a deep limit to her work. I turn to Beauvoir neither to extend this limit nor to advocate for colonizing perception. As I will discuss in subsequent chapters, one of my primary aims is to consider the way the temporality of feminine existence is bound to colonial operations of race, gender, and time. My reading of Beauvoir is rooted in an acknowledgment of the racial and colonial problems and limits of her description of becoming a woman. My reading of Beauvoir and what she says (or doesn't say) and does begins from the position that in saying nothing about racial difference and racism, the text speaks about and performs the work of whiteness. In this chapter I have made a choice not to advance a particularly explicit account of whiteness in relation to the temporality of feminine existence. Instead, I develop the preliminary conceptual apparatus that I will complicate and develop throughout the rest of the book in order to account for the relation between race, gender, and sexual domination as a matter of how we live time. I first turn to Beauvoir because I find her discussion of the relation between temporality and feminine existence to be instructive and one worth critically developing in relation to colonial racism. The latter task is the work I undertake in chapters 2 and 3 most specifically.

Here I first advance a general theoretical gesture to a feminist reconsideration of how to think the relation between gender and time by drawing on Beauvoir's account of the relation between temporality and feminine existence. I account for the dominant reading of Beauvoir, drawing specifically on Judith Butler's reading of Beauvoir, in order to shift how we think about gender and temporality in the context of The Second Sex.[1] I look to Butler's reading for several reasons. I find it to exemplify the broader reception of Beauvoir in contemporary feminist theory. Although the efforts of feminist phenomenologists and Beauvoir scholars often challenge Butler's reading, I nevertheless think Butler's influence in feminist theory, especially in the Anglo-American context, suggests that her reading of Beauvoir has left a remarkable footprint on how (or whether) feminists read Beauvoir. Subsequently I trace Beauvoir's discussion of temporality in volume 2 of The Second Sex in order to show that she understands the temporality of waiting—what I refer to as a passive present—to be an underlying structure of women's existence and subordination. Although Beauvoir occasionally engages the theme of temporality in volume 1, on a close reading, Beauvoir's concern with the lived experience of temporality, which is also my concern, is formative to her descriptive account of becoming a woman in volume 2. Of course, it would be an error to claim that there is not a connection between volumes 1 and 2 of The Second Sex. But my interest in the discussion of temporality in volume 2 is meant to address how, in a world where feminine existence is constituted (which is what Beauvoir addresses in volume 1), a woman experiences her self and the world. My reading of Beauvoir brings me to my own development of her claim about the relation between the temporality of feminine existence and sexual domination.

On Becoming

Most readings of Beauvoir do not pay close attention to the theme of temporality that permeates volume 2 of *The Second Sex*, entitled *Lived Experience*.[2] Instead, the dominant reading of temporality locates the temporality of gender in Beauvoir's famous sentence, "One is not born, but rather becomes, a woman" (1949, 13, my translation).[3] Judith Butler's account of Beauvoir's sentence is a notable example of such a reading. For Butler, Beauvoir's sentence is significant because of the temporal claim it makes about gender as a process of acquisition:

> Gender must be understood as a modality of taking on or realizing possibilities, a process of interpreting the body, giving it cultural form. In other words, to be a woman is to become a woman; it is not a matter of acquiescing to a fixed ontological status, in which case one could be born a woman, but, rather, an active process of appropriating, interpreting, and reinterpreting received cultural possibilities. (1986, 36)

This reading of Beauvoir's notion of becoming as an active temporal process of acquisition is not only consistently present in Butler's work but is also formative to her performative theory of gender.[4] Thus, Butler advances an account of the relation between gender and temporality that uses Beauvoir's notion of becoming as the temporality of gender.

Before *Gender Trouble* (1990), Butler argues that Beauvoir's famous sentence, and more specifically the notion of becoming contained in it, "distinguishes sex from gender and suggests that gender is an aspect of identity gradually acquired" (1986, 35). For Butler, this offers an important account of gender as "both choice and acculturation" (37). Understanding gender as acquired and thoroughly cultural undermines the alleged causal relation between sex and gender, and underscores gender as a temporal phenomenon. Hence, as Butler argues, we see that gender "is not temporally discrete because gender is not originated at some point in time after which it is fixed in form" (39). It "is not traceable to a definable origin precisely because it is itself an originating activity incessantly taking place" (39). These Butlerian claims about gender all stem from Beauvoir's notion of becoming. As Butler sees it, the notion of becoming found in Beauvoir's famous sentence discloses not only the temporal movement of gender as a continuous way of taking up and responding to cultural norms but also, more generally, shows that gendered subjectivity is temporal through and through. In "Performative Acts and Gender Constitution," Butler further elaborates on this reading of Beauvoir. We learn that for Butler, becoming a woman means gender "is an identity tenuously constituted in time," moving "the conception of gender off the ground of a substantial model of identity to one that requires a conception of gender as a constituted *social temporality*" (1988, 519, 520). That one becomes a woman is, on Butler's reading of Beauvoir, to say that gender is constructed in time.

This reading of Beauvoir later becomes Butler's own temporal conception of gender. In *Gender Trouble* ([1990] 1999), Butler is critical of Beauvoir, claiming that she adopts the Cartesian mind/body dualism, thereby taking the sexed body to be a natural fact that is indifferent to signification. Yet Butler still praises the notion of becoming: "If there is something right in Beauvoir's claim that one is not born, but rather *becomes* a woman," Butler writes, "it follows that *woman* itself is a term in process, a becoming, a constructing that cannot rightfully be said to originate or to end" (1986, 45). From this reading of Beauvoir's notion of becoming, Butler advances her own conception of gender as repetition, a temporal process of continual renewal amidst a social world. Butler writes: "It is, for Beauvoir, never possible finally to become a woman, as if there were a *telos* that governs the process of acculturation and construction. Gender is the repeated stylization of the body, a set of repeated acts within a highly rigid regulatory frame that congeal over time to produce the appearance of substance, of a natural sort of being" (45). As a derivative of Beauvoir's notion of becoming, Butler claims the gendered subject is produced through "a stylized repetition of acts" or through the "reenactment and reexperiencing of a set of meanings already socially established" (191). This view leads Butler to argue for "a conception of gender as a constituted *social temporality*," a conception Butler previously ascribed to Beauvoir (191). However, Butler also differentiates her temporal conception of gender from Beauvoir's, arguing that the sexed body is constituted through the repetition of "words, acts, gestures, and desire" (185). The sexed body is an effect of gender, Butler insists; that is, sex is a product of the repetition of gender. Or, to put it another way, repetition is the performative dimension of gender that constructs, guarantees, and destabilizes the gendered subject as well as the sexed body. This leads Butler to claim that "gender is an identity tenuously constituted in time" (191).

Butler's temporal account of gender is not necessarily wrong. Feminists have long insisted that gender is not a determined, biological reality; instead, they advocate for an account of gender that takes seriously its temporal character and production. Butler's notion of gender as performative repetition, historical accounts of gender (see Bederman 1996), or a sociological theory of "doing gender" (see West and Zimmerman 1987), all underscore gender as an ideological temporal process. The persistence of feminist conceptions of gender as temporal suggests that at the very least there is something agreeable with Butler's claim that gender identity is temporally constituted. But is Butler's reading of Beauvoir the best possible reading? Does Beauvoir take becoming to be the crucial temporal character of gender subjectivity?

Sara Heinämaa is the feminist philosopher who has most explicitly challenged Butler's reading of Beauvoir's famous sentence. Heinämaa argues that Butler misinterprets Beauvoir's notion of becoming by reading the born/becoming distinction as the sex/gender distinction. According to Heinämaa, Butler consistently presents Beauvoir's work "as a theory about the socio-cultural production of gender (feminine, woman), presupposing a factual basis in nature and outside all signification (female)" (1997, 29). In contrast, Heinämaa argues that the sex/gender distinction is not present in Beauvoir's work such that becoming cannot and does not indicate, as Butler thinks, a temporal process of social acquisition and cannot therefore translate as a social constructionist theory of gender. For Heinämaa, insofar as the sex/gender distinction is the framework through which Butler reads becoming, she overlooks the phenomenological aim of *The Second Sex*. In response to Butler's misreading, Heinämaa suggests Beauvoir's intention is to describe the meaning of "woman" and "femininity" as a lived corporeal style. From this view, we must think of Beauvoir as attempting to address how woman, as a body-subject, realizes herself as she is intertwined with the world. As such, becoming raises the phenomenological question of possibility: how is it possible that one becomes a woman and becomes a woman as a feminine existence?

Following Heinämaa, becoming is not an achievement that produces a particular kind of body but rather refers to a particular way of assuming one's embodied existence. When Beauvoir claims that one becomes a woman, she is not making a claim about gender. Rather, she is asking about how woman, as a stylized mode of being, is realized. That one becomes a woman does not mean woman is an effect of repetitive acts, but in contrast, becoming gestures to the way womanhood, its values and meanings, is "a structure of . . . being, not a specific object, attribute, or a collection" of acts (Heinämaa 2003, 302).

Heinämaa's (1996) notion of "woman as style" draws on Merleau-Ponty's notion of style.[5] For Merleau-Ponty, style is a distinctive, corporeal aesthetic, a particular way of inhabiting the world that is disclosed in our bodily gestures. Similar to how a painter develops an aesthetic mode of expression through which she crafts a unique and recognizable perspective in her artwork, a corporeal style discloses an individual mode of existence. Just as an artist's style generates an aesthetic that renders a work as her work, a corporeal style renders me as me. In this sense, style is a bodily aesthetic that makes one intelligible as a particular subject in a given social milieu. On this view, becoming a woman refers not to the way subjective actions congeal over time to produce an intelligible gender subject "woman," but rather refers to the way a woman realizes herself through particular modalities of bodily comportment and conditions of one's bodily existence in the world. In other words, one becomes a woman not as a causal outcome of biology or the mere result of a social construction, but through the way one assumes the particularity of her bodily existence in a concrete situation (see also Mann 2014). To become a woman is thus to realize a corporeal style—a particular way of acting, moving, talking, and so on— that is at once individual and collective.

Because the phenomenological view rejects the nature/culture distinction, the corporeal style of feminine existence, its disclosure of the *who* of a person, is neither natural nor merely cultural; it is a habituation that unfolds in and as the lived experience of a body in a world. As such, the phenomenological reading pushes back against Butler's constructionist reading of the body, suggesting that to become a woman does not mean that one acquires a gendered body, but rather it is to suggest that woman is taken up in and through the living body. Heinämaa, however, also accounts for woman as realized and altered in repetition and as sedimentation of earlier intentional acts, suggesting that former embodied actions open up and provoke future actions. Yet in contrast to Butler, Heinämaa argues that repetition and sedimentation refer to a temporal unfolding of the living body. In this sense, becoming a woman is still a temporal process, but a woman is not produced. Rather, she realizes herself through the accumulation of a past that is repeated and modified in order to actualize a distinct way of going toward the world. (I build on the phenomenological reading of sedimentation and temporal accumulation in chapter 4, where I discuss how a phenomenological account of sedimentation and habituation offers a better way to think the relation between the body and the actualization of normative gender subjectivity as it takes shapes through structures and experiences of racialized, sexualized power.) Ultimately, though, the key distinction between Butler's constructionist account of gender and Heinämaa's phenomenological account of becoming a woman is the way in which the body is understood. From the constructionist perspective, the body is constructed through repetitive acts, whereas the phenomenological view underscores the way gendered style actualizes through the entanglement of physiological processes and the sociocultural context in which those processes are lived. By shifting the philosophical framework through which we read Beauvoir, Heinämaa offers a phenomenological reading of becoming that emphasizes that woman is realized by a body-subject in and over time. To become a woman is to subjectively assume a particular style of existence.

Although I take seriously Heinämaa's insistence that *The Second Sex* is not a constructionist account of gender, she nevertheless commits to becoming as the temporal claim in *The Second Sex*. She does not challenge the claim that becoming is Beauvoir's temporal understanding of woman. Certainly, becoming is the temporal claim in the famous sentence of *The Second Sex*, but there is another way to understand the temporality of subjectivity in Beauvoir's account. As Merleau-Ponty's phenomenological account of subjectivity suggests, "Subjectivity is not in time because it takes up or lives time" (2012, 466). Given this claim, and given that Beauvoir returns to the theme of temporality throughout her massive descriptive account of becoming a woman, it is important to consider whether or not an understanding of woman as in time is how Beauvoir conceives of the relation between temporality and woman.[6] In particular, what does one understand when Merleau-Ponty's claim is read in relation to Beauvoir's descriptive account of becoming a woman in *The Second Sex*? Might we want to think about how a woman lives time? More specifically, insofar as phenomenology accounts for the lived experience of time, it is important to ask: How is woman a particular lived experience of time? How is woman, as a body-subject, realized as temporality? How is feminine existence a disclosure of a temporal style?

The Second Sex as a Feminist Phenomenology of Temporality

Beauvoir advances a feminist phenomenology of temporality as she advances a feminist phenomenology of gender in *The Second Sex*. In Beauvoir's perspective, becoming a woman is to live time in a particular way. What this means is that Beauvoir takes becoming to be the realization of a temporal style, the details and consequences of which will become clearer in what follows. That Beauvoir understands becoming a woman to require a lived experience of time means on the one hand that gender is lived time and on the other hand that Beauvoir takes gender and temporality to be co-constitutive, a claim I take to be central to a feminist phenomenology of temporality.

Beauvoir's discussion of temporality revolves around the notions of immanence and transcendence, and the classical phenomenological account of the triadic temporal structure of experience. Beauvoir (1976, 2005) introduces the concepts of immanence and transcendence as a way to underscore the ambiguity of the human condition as facticity and freedom. As such, immanence and transcendence refer to a general structure of human existence.[7] In *The Second Sex*, Beauvoir understands immanence and transcendence to structure human temporality but suggests that this general structure is bifurcated by sexual difference such that men and women are denied unmediated access to the whole structure of human temporality. This means that although Beauvoir underscores that women and men live both immanence and transcendence, she ultimately argues that there is a significant difference in how they live these temporalities. Thus, consistent with classical phenomenology, Beauvoir understands temporality to constitute the horizon of subjective experience and to structure one's being-in-the-world, but she breaks with the tradition by claiming that temporality is entangled with the particularity of becoming a woman.

More specifically, Beauvoir argues that a woman's subjectivity is characterized by the temporality of immanence through ruptures in the triadic structure of time, which institute a cyclical embodiment of the present that is constitutive of a woman as a particular kind of gendered being. This embodied present leaves Beauvoir to lament that a woman's "whole existence is a waiting since she is enclosed in the limbo of immanence and contingency" (2010, 649). For Beauvoir, waiting is a temporal hiatus between the past and future, which means that waiting is a distinct experience of the present as passive; it neither reaches back to the past nor toward a future.

In order to understand how a woman comes to embody time in this distinct way, it is first necessary to consider why, for Beauvoir, "becoming a woman is breaking with the past, without recourse" (2010, 391). Beauvoir accounts for three distinct breaks or ruptures with the past, which coincide with three existentially significant developmental events: girlhood, heterosexual initiation, and marriage. These ruptures in time annex a woman into the universe of men, to the world that is for men, such that she comes to exist as their plaything. The ruptures are thus heterosexist in character insofar as they come to create and solidify a woman's situation as a relative existence.

Beginning with her account of girlhood, Beauvoir suggests that a girl lives "detached from her childhood past" where "the present is for her only a transition. . . . In a more or less disguised way, her youth is consumed by waiting. She is waiting for Man" (2010, 341). This detachment from the past throws a girl into an anticipatory temporality of waiting, which begins her immersion into the world of men and a conversion of her existence as for men. This anticipatory temporality is strikingly different than the anticipatory temporality that drives the Heideggerian Dasein into existence. For Martin Heidegger (1962), anticipation is what propels human existence toward the future; it is a movement beyond oneself, a temporal mode that is integral to one's existence. However, the girl's anticipatory temporality is a temporal stasis, and as such it begins to diminish her claim to a future. In contrast to childhood, where the girl's temporal horizon, like that of a boy's, is an open structure that seamlessly integrates the past and present toward a future, the temporality of waiting is a temporal suspension achieved by a break with the past. No longer a mere child, the girl is suspended in the time between her past structured by transcendence and a future structured by immanence. This is a temporal conversion that genders her existence in a meaningful way. She no longer experiences herself as a child. She now feels herself to be a girl, and this conversion is imposed on her through a shift in her relation to time. This temporal shift marks an important conflict "between her originary claim to be subject, activity, and freedom, on the one hand and, on the other, her erotic tendencies and the social pressure to assume her self as a passive object" (Beauvoir 2010, 348). Thus, in girlhood, waiting is the temporal conversion that underlies sexual objectification and severs the girl's claim to freedom.

This conflict is resolved through "a new occurrence that creates a rupture with the past": heterosexual initiation (Beauvoir 2010, 383). Unlike the girl whose freedom is tenuous, the first experience of heterosexual sex in a misogynist world is, Beauvoir claims, a temporal conversion of the girl's experience of herself as a tenuous subject to an object. While girlhood left her waiting for her future as a man's object, heterosexual sex inaugurates "a hiatus between yesterday and tomorrow" wherein the temporality of waiting becomes the temporality of the present (391). In this sense, the present is a temporal isolation insofar as it is not a present that is bound to the past or future but is instead an interruption in the triadic structure of time. The temporal hiatus anchors a girl to the present, which is the experience of time that comes to characterize the temporal horizon of a woman. She is hurled into a present that reaches neither back to the past nor toward the future. As such, the present is marked by passivity, a lifeless temporal mode that severs a woman's claim to transcendence.

For Beauvoir, marriage is the developmental and existential event that reifies the temporal structure of womanhood as a passive present. Although historically it is generally only the most privileged women for whom marriage is the significant event that institutes feminine existence, in my reading, what is important about Beauvoir's claim about marriage is that it underscores that a temporal conversion is central to domination. The event of marriage sediments the temporal conversion of domination; it achieves the shift from lived time as an open structure to a closed one. For Beauvoir, the married woman "breaks with the past more or less brutally" because "she is annexed to her husband's universe" (2010, 442). The difference between this rupture and the ones before is that now a woman exists in a very concrete way for a particular man. This realization of her relative existence guarantees and deepens a woman's suspension in the present as a concrete temporal limbo. When she becomes a part of her husband's universe, she becomes a stranger to her own past and her own future; she is incorporated into his time. This leaves a woman exiled in a present that refers only to itself. Indeed, as Beauvoir says, a married woman is "lost in the middle of a world to which no aim calls her, abandoned in an icy present" (487). Without recourse to her past and without unmediated access to a future of her own making, a woman is trapped in and thus assumes a passive present. She is frozen in time. This particular experience of an entrapment in the present is, for Beauvoir, how a woman's existence is a waiting. Steeped in the present, a woman embodies a temporal state of repose or passivity. As in girlhood, a woman waits for the temporal justification of her existence. A woman lives the future and the past vicariously through her husband because he "posits ends and projects paths to them . . . he spills over the present and opens up the future" (73). Consequently, while the temporal ruptures are significant to becoming a woman insofar as they institute the passive present, the temporality of woman is, for Beauvoir, the closed, rigid experience of an icy present.[8]

Importantly, the confinement to the present is one of the ways in which Beauvoir understands a woman to be relegated to immanence inasmuch as the "present is eternal, useless, and hopeless" (2010, 475). A woman's relation to time is redundant. Living "every day . . . like the previous one," time "seems to be going around in circles without going anywhere" (475, 644). As Penelope Deutscher argues, this repetition "impoverishes a woman's relation to time" insofar as a woman habituates herself to an eternal present (2008, 97). In making the redundancy of time habitual, in living the present over and over again, a woman loses an autonomous claim to transcendence, a relationship to freedom where the past and present tend toward one's own future.[9] Thus, feminine existence, in Beauvoir's critical view, is refused a dynamic and open relation to and experience of time. The woman waits for her life to begin, her days to end and begin again, her chores and tasks to be repeated.

Interestingly, Lisa Guenther's phenomenology of the temporality of supermax confinement suggests that the temporal structure of waiting is central to a prison temporality that "reinforces inmates' dependence on prison authorities to receive even the most basic rights and privileges" (2013, 196). In prison, waiting to do nothing, waiting for release, waiting for the arrival of a meal, of a letter, a book, is the experience of a loss of control of one's own time. The persistence and intense experience of waiting is, as Guenther puts, "the implicit message" that "you are no longer in charge of your own time" (196). Although it would be a mistake to equate a woman's experience of waiting with that of the inmate who endures intensive confinement, Guenther's account of prison temporality does illuminate a carceral logic at the heart of the temporality of feminine existence. Her account raises the question: to what extent is feminine existence a life sentence, a particular mode of confinement that isolates a woman from a meaningful existence?

In the final chapter of this book, I will come back to Guenther's account of prison temporality as a way to think a feminist temporal politics of resistance, but here I want to underscore that feminine existence undermines one's capacity to, as Guenther puts, "*do* time, to make time, to comport themselves as living, temporal subjects" (2013, 199). It is a gendered sentence to a life of confinement that is an enabling condition of and is itself a means of sexual domination. This point is not meant to suggest that there are not life sentences bound to other modes of gendered existence. Queer, gender-nonconforming, and trans lives endure harsh sentences in relation to incarceration specifically and to society's carceral logics more generally (Mogul, Ritchie, and Whitlock 2011; Stanley, Smith, and McDonald 2015). My point here is to draw attention to the way the temporality of feminine existence in particular functions as a means of gendered subjectification as sexual domination. (And, arguably, the imposition of this temporality produces and sustains other modes of gendered temporality as domination.)

To become a woman in the misogynist style—that is, to assume a feminine existence—is to take up a particular relation to time through relentless imposition and existential burden. It is to assume or embody a passive present, a temporal mode of waiting, such that a woman's redundant experience of the present becomes her. She is the present. Feminine existence as a particular gendered existence is thus taken up as an existential project through temporality. Certainly some women are burdened by such an existence more than others, some women resist such an existence, and some women find comfort in such an existence. For Beauvoir, however, the operation of the temporality of feminine existence affects all those who are set up to become women in a misogynist world, regardless of whether the temporality is always realized by a subject herself.

Ultimately a feminist phenomenology of temporality suggests that how we live time is a central way that gender structures and is imposed on us and how temporality operates as both a structure and experience of subordination. From this view, we understand that gendered subjectivity and gender oppression are not merely phenomena in time but temporalize and thus are lived as and through particular experiences of time. Beauvoir's account thus suggests that temporality is gendered and is part of the way gender is constituted. She shows how gender intervenes with the general human temporality of immanence and transcendence. It is not that a woman is immanence as a man is transcendence, but rather that the general structure of human temporality is entangled with the social and historical mediation and valuation of living bodies. In contrast to the classical phenomenological emphasis on a general structure of human temporality, Beauvoir's account of temporality in *The Second Sex* takes seriously the way in which the particularity of the historical and social phenomenon of gender mediates the generality of lived time. As she sees it, temporality does not precede gender. Insofar as subjectivity is realized through gender, Beauvoir claims that how we live time is entangled with the reality of becoming a gendered being. For Beauvoir, a dynamic experience of time, an experience in which the future is opened up by the past and present, is not lived by women because their material conditions do not grant it. In contrast to classical phenomenology, Beauvoir argues that a triadic temporal horizon is not a given feature of human existence but is instead conferred by the material conditions in which one lives. Beauvoir's phenomenology of temporality not only makes it problematic to posit a genderless, primordial structure of lived time but also demands an understanding of gender as bound to the experience of time.

What her account misses—and it is no small omission—is that it is not only the particularity of gender that structures temporality but also that gendered temporality is already entangled with the operation of other distinct social and historical temporalities. Before I consider these omissions, I want to consider what Beauvoir's feminist phenomenology of temporality underscores about the relation between temporality and sexual domination. In no way do I think her account is the end of the story of this relation, but I do think it offers a helpful conceptual framework from which to address the temporal structure of racialized heteropatriarchal sexual domination. I will complicate this structure and my discussion of the temporality of sexual domination in relation to colonial temporalities in chapter 2.

The Temporalization of Sexual Domination

The social control of women in a heteropatriarchal society manifests in how the very seconds, minutes, and hours of an individual woman's days, weeks, and years are spent. Women spend more time doing domestic work and labor associated with keeping house; women are also consumed with unreciprocated emotional labor, spending ample time listening to, caring for, tending to, and being consumed by the egos, feelings, and lives of others, especially men; and women working in low-wage labor are also subjected to regimes of temporality that require them to work expediently, for long hours, and without breaks. Women are interrupted more often than men such that their time is punctuated. Women who take up the disciplinary regimes governing contemporary heteropatriarchal Western standards of beauty spend a significant amount of time on their appearance. Indeed, because of the intense scrutiny that women are subjected to regarding their appearance, many women labor for beauty, spending numerous hours each day in front of the mirror before they can go spend even more of their time tending to the demands of others. The account of feminine existence as a passive present I have offered here is achieved through the gendering of time that results from the various forms of labor and social practices like the ones I have just mentioned. There is no doubt in my mind that there are numerous social disciplinary practices and forms of labor, which operate as nuanced modes of hetero desire and eroticism, that generate the temporality of feminine existence. There is also no doubt that there are even practices that produce liberatory experiences of time, however difficult they may be to realize or hold on to. However, rather than documenting the various ways women live time differently and through what means these temporal experiences are realized, to give an account of feminine existence as a passive present is to name the overarching temporality of domination that structures the lives of those who are or are taken to be women in a heteropatriarchal society.

It is crucial to note that the account of the temporality of feminine existence that Beauvoir develops is marked by existential harm. In patriarchal contexts, to break with the past without recourse is to assume an existence that is merely relative, that is shackled to immanence, and that is torn—a tear between one's past and one's future that is lived as a self-rupturing, a brutal tear with what one was and who one can be. Yet as Beauvoir conceives it, this temporal break is oppressive because it severs a woman's claim to freedom and also oppressive specifically through its particular sexualized character. As she discusses the temporal (and developmental) conversions that make one a woman, Beauvoir accounts for the girl's erotic activities and sexual initiation as vicious, discusses the young girl as wounded, shamed, and torn, and understands the married woman to be brutalized by marriage. Hence, the heteroerotic character of the harm suggests that the temporality of femininity is itself a mode of sexual domination. Beauvoir's account of temporality shows that a woman's lived relation to time conditions a woman's bodily existence in the world as thinglike, a mode of existence that is profoundly marked by an erotic existence that is for men. In breaking with the past and assuming a never-ending, passive present, the temporality of a woman is that which constrains, confines, and encloses her in the world. But beyond this, Beauvoir also claims that the temporal cage of the passive present preempts a woman from experiencing herself as a sexual subject. Instead, she is petrified into a sexualized idol. When a woman is abandoned in and takes up the present, she lives a temporal paralysis that turns her into sexualized prey. Through her particular relation to and embodiment of time, a woman assumes an existence in which she is ready and able to be put to sexual use.

In her groundbreaking article "Throwing Like a Girl," Iris Marion Young argues that in Western patriarchal societies, there is a "particular style of bodily comportment that is typical of feminine existence," which entails a relation to space through which women are "inhibited, confined, positioned, and objectified" (1980, 141). For Young, the more a girl or woman assumes this relation to space, the more she takes herself to be a feminine existence, and the more she experiences herself as confined and immobile. One of the central ways this spatial confinement is produced is through sexual domination. That girls and women are, in patriarchal societies, taken to be sexual objects, as body-subjects capable of being and who are put to use for others, they "tend to project an existential barrier around them . . . in order to keep the other at a distance" (154). A woman's limited experience of space is an effort to guard against the possibility of violation because "to go beyond that space is to enter an arena where her body is in danger of being violated" (Cahill 2001, 158). The spatiality of feminine existence is thus one that simultaneously positions a woman as sexually violable by anchoring her to space and through which a woman lives out her sexually violability by restricting her existence in space. This particular lived experience of space is therefore central to complicated, patriarchal processes of sexual subjectification. Through her relation to space, a woman is constituted as a sexualized subject for others.

Although Beauvoir does not spell this out explicitly, the temporal mode of feminine existence is central to this process of sexual subjectification. What she does do, however, is underscore a requisite suspension of a girl's transcendence through heteromasculinist eroticism, from which it is possible to perceive the relation between the embodied temporality of feminine existence and sexual subjectification and domination in *The Second Sex*. For Beauvoir, "society even requires woman to make herself an erotic object . . . not to reveal her as an autonomous individual but, on the contrary, to cut her from transcendence so as to offer her as a prey to male desire" (2010, 572). This image of a woman as prey is telling in relation to temporality. To live as prey is to be potentially hunted. It is to have one's existence reduced to a hunter's world-making projects. For a woman to live as prey suggests that she is enveloped in her predator's world. Thus, when a woman becomes a waiting, when she is abandoned in an icy present, she lives a profound existential dependency, a dependency that is fundamentally and violently sexualized. In being reduced to and confined to a passive present, she is stripped of her human capacity to be a subject who simultaneously constitutes and is constituted by time, and in turn, a woman is in or positioned by time. This positioning turns her into sexual prey. Such temporal paralysis is a necessary structure of sexual domination. (As I will discuss in chapter 5, this temporal paralysis, being frozen in time, shares much in common with the temporal effects of trauma.)

A concrete example will help illustrate the temporal structure of sexual domination I am describing. Bonnie Mann's (2012) analysis of creepiness highlights the way experiences of time are central to sexual subjectification and domination. Creepiness is the all-too-common experience that many young women have while at the gym or while waiting in line at the grocery store, and some guy slyly undresses her with his eyes. It is when a man presses himself up against a young woman or places his hand on her arm or thigh so he can cop a feel. It is when, while walking home in broad daylight, a group of men reduce a woman to her body and attempt to get her attention with their sexualized stares. On Mann's account, creepiness fails to register as sexual harassment because it is an ordinary operation of gender and exceeds the legal conception of sexual harassment. But this does not make it any less nefarious; in fact, it might make it all the worse. Mann accounts for the primary harm of the creeper, the man who creeps and enacts creepiness, as a sexualized theft of time. She argues that the temporal theft is a product of the creeper's entitled intentionality: he is "already in the mode of 'I-regard-you-as-fuckable'" when he encounters a woman (26). In this mode, the creeper reduces a woman to his world, which forecloses her capacity to comport herself as a temporal subject. For example, in the instance of an experience of street harassment, a woman's future is interrupted as she is hurled into the present moment of being rendered fuckable by the street harasser. Her thoughts are no longer on where she is going and how she is getting there, how she feels about the weather, what she wants to eat for dinner, or whatever else may be preoccupying her inner world. Instead, she is focused on that moment. Excuse me. What did he just say? Fuck you. Should I snap back? Am I in danger? Is he following me? Her capacity to exist beyond herself becomes reduced to that present. Accordingly, as Mann puts it, the temporal harm the creeper enacts is that the woman's agency is consumed by the creeper's "dominant intentional mood" (30). His mood compels "her subjective capacities to be-in-relation to him in a field whose possibilities he affectively controls" (26). The woman's ability to negotiate the encounter on her terms is preempted by the fact that the woman has become positioned in the creeper's temporal field. Her relation to her future devolves into an experience of a passive present in the moment that she is put to use for him.

Of course, she might be able to conjure up a resistant response and talk back, which would allow her to build a world of her own again, but this comes after the fact that her time, as her own, has already been called into question. Even if she can find a response, the logic of misogyny prevents the response from fully rebuilding the woman's world because the response itself heightens her vulnerability. As Kate Manne explains in *Down Girl* (2018), misogyny's mood of entitlement entails the threat of force when a man does not get what he wants from a woman, whether that be her attention, her body, her love and adoration, her submission, or even her absence from a male-dominated space. In a misogynist encounter, a woman's refusal to yield her time to a man is structured by, as Manne argues, a differential norm of giving that subjects the woman to the potential of a violent backlash. Accordingly, "If he [a man] is not given his due," if the woman refuses the creeper's gestures, if she snaps back at him to reclaim her time, "he may then be permitted to take . . . to forcibly seize" what he feels he is due just because he is a man. She will be perceived "to have stolen something from him" even though it will be she who has been harmed (2018, 117).

Fiona Vera-Grey's empirical phenomenological analysis of young women's experience of men's sexual intrusion in public space illustrates the gravity of living this sexualized theft of time regularly, repeatedly, or even as a possibility. To avoid or cope with men's sexual intrusion or its possibility, the women in Vera-Grey's research "acknowledged a conscious adaptation of behavior, movement and bodily posture" that decreased their freedom of movement (2017, 133). This emphasis on the spatial practices and restrictions imposed through men's sexual intrusion underscores the classic feminist analysis of the spatiality of sexual domination and feminine embodiment. My point here, following Mann's concern with the theft of time, is not only that the limited freedom of movement is also a relation to time but also that the harm of sexual domination is a temporal harm. Moreover, understanding the passive present as a sexualized theft of time helps us think about how sexual domination is encrusted into the life of a woman. The particular relation to and embodied experience of the passive present makes a woman a sexualized subject for others. Whereas a woman can, at least with training, begin to perceive how she takes up space, how she moves in space, and how she does or does not use her body in space, temporality is an inconspicuous dimension of a woman's subjective experience. How she lives time does not give itself to the same kind of immediacy that her spatiality does. In this sense, the presence of sexual domination is inconspicuously lodged in a woman's existence through temporality. Temporality therefore tacitly conspires to generate and structure a woman's existence as sexually violable. That temporality is a structure of existence means that this conspiracy is existentially deep.

This conspiracy between temporality and sexual domination is telling with regard to the temporal structure of rape culture. While the explicit harm of rape culture is that a girl or woman is continuously and ubiquitously subject to sexual violence or its possibilities, the implicit harm is that one is continuously reduced to the present, not as a subjective presence but as a subject to be taken. This sexualized theft of time—turning a woman into a passive present, becoming a woman as a passive present—is a deep and pervasive existential injury. Inasmuch as rape culture thrives on the implicit injury that one is always potentially prey, a girl or woman is always potentially huntable; girls and women are perpetually subject to the temporal harm of the eternal present—the embodied experience of living in an almost inescapable temporal cage, a cage that makes one sexual prey. As we will see in the next chapter, colonial racialization undermines this experience as a subject to be taken in severe ways. A black woman, for instance, will still be subjected to the theft of time, yet because her positioning in the colonial racial schema undermines her intelligibility as a woman, the theft of time she experiences is not as a subject to be taken but as an object to be eliminated.

Today, however, it is the case that girls and women (of various racial and ethnic groups) do take up space and experience their body-space in expansive and dynamic ways. They are encouraged to and do pursue sports, they are encouraged to be and are concerned about their education and careers, and occasionally they have some institutional and social support to participate in world-making activities, all efforts that Beauvoir would recognize as transcendence. Yet by no means are their possibilities and world-making pursuits free of constraint. Women are still barred from institutions and careers, subject to gender policing in sports, restricted in their gender expression, and hold little formal and informal security in their person. But what has been even much more recalcitrant is the persistent representation and understanding of girls and women as sexual prey. In fact, in *Hunting Girls*, an analysis of popular representations of young women as violent, Kelly Oliver suggests that as girls and women have gained access to the masculine domain, particularly the domain of violence, they have only become more mired in their status as sexual prey. For Oliver, although girls and women can now be predators, and serious ones at that, contemporary "hunting girls" "still get it as much, or more, than they give" (2016, 115). As women have gained access to the role of the predator, Oliver suggests, their role as sexual prey is profoundly reified. But more than this, the temporality of feminine existence is still assumed by girls and women because it remains central to being intelligible and desirable as a woman in a heteromasculinist world. As Beauvoir tells us, the difficulty in undoing this temporality and its existential harm is the reality that it also becomes a means of pleasure and empowerment for a woman. It is not that the temporality of feminine existence is simply imposed on a girl or a woman but that it actualizes as an existential harm, and bestows recognition and access to the world.

The temporality of feminine existence thus confers intelligibility, approval, and quasi-empowerment. Moreover, even when feminine existence is deeply resisted, the passive present still creeps into a woman's experience. Beauvoir makes this evident in her discussion of the independent woman, a woman who has resisted becoming a vassal and finds some success in making a world for herself as a subject. While the "vassal woman" has resigned her sexual agency to the world of men, the independent woman chooses "not resignation but combat" in effort to resist her sexual subjectification (Beauvoir 2010, 726, 727). The trouble, though, is that even if the independent woman succeeds in authoring her own sexual activities, her "victory remains ambiguous" because "according to public opinion, it is the man who conquers, who *has* the woman. It does not accept that she can, like the man, assume her desires: she is their prey" (730). Independence, resistance, and rejection of feminine passivity and submission by a woman herself are thus not enough to remove oneself from the passive present.

Temporality and Gendered Existence

This account of gender as lived time and of feminine existence as structured by a passive present through which sexual domination creeps its way into a woman's existence is central to the rest of this inquiry. I have returned to Beauvoir because she offers a way to change the feminist discussion about gender and time. Her phenomenological account of temporality as a structure of gender subjectivity, and in turn her account of gendered temporality, is key to understanding how girls and women and the prevailing schema of gender are bound to sexual domination. By drawing on Beauvoir in this way, it is possible to examine how time is deployed in the gendering of subjective life—how relations to time, lived experiences of time, become sly ways in which individuals live and embody violently oppressive gender ideologies. Following this Beauvoirian conception of the temporality of feminine existence, in what immediately follows I examine how colonial legacies are central to the operation of the temporality of feminine existence today. I do so to consider how we inherit racialized histories of rape vis-à-vis temporality in the lived experience of normative gender.

Part I

The Past

There is no question of expressing eternal truths here, but of describing the common ground from which all singular feminine existence stems.

—Simone de Beauvoir, *The Second Sex*

2

Sexualized Racism and the Politics of Time

As I began to work on this chapter, former Oklahoma City police officer Daniel Holtzclaw was convicted of committing numerous rapes and sexual assaults against thirteen African American women ranging in age from seventeen to fifty-seven. He was sentenced to 263 years in prison. The morning after Holtzclaw's conviction, I sat in my office some forty-five minutes away from Oklahoma City and read a now well-circulated statement from the closing argument of the prosecutor, District Attorney Lori McConnell: "He didn't choose CEOs or soccer moms. He chose women he could count on not telling what he was doing. He counted on the fact that no one would believe them and no one would care" (Brandes 2015). What McConnell was actually saying, of course, was that Holtzclaw chose his victims because they were *black* women. They were not white soccer moms who, in the eyes of the law, the state, and many residents of Oklahoma, are respectable women, quasi-protected women, the kind of women a cop does not target to rape. That Holtzclaw was convicted by an all-white jury in one of the most conservative states in America was for some a huge victory against the state's patriarchal white supremacy and a small redemption for the survivors. Although I believe the question of personal redemption is one that can only be answered by each of the thirteen black women, I was and still am suspicious of the sentiment of victory. How much did this verdict change the state's use of rape against women of color? How, if at all, did it shift the state's racialized heterogender commitments?

The use of rape against women of color has a particularly pernicious history. The dehumanization and trauma endured by the thirteen black women for the pleasure and power of Holtzclaw is but one event in a deep history of state violence against women of color in the United States. Numerous feminist scholars have documented the disturbingly multiple, intricate, explicit, and nuanced ways that colonial conquest sanctions and uses rape against nonwhite, non-Western, immigrant, and indigenous women at rates far higher, and often in ways far more brutal, than white

Western women (Davis 1981; Gunn Allen 1986; Collins 2004; Smith 2005; Deer 2015; Ritchie 2017). This reality is even more sinister when one takes seriously that such rape has been systematically concealed and justified by racist colonial governments and their (white) citizens (Davis 1981; Crenshaw 1991; Smith 2005; Deer 2015). In the contemporary United States, with the exception of American Indian victims, the rape of women by men is largely an intraracial phenomenon that occurs not through the appendages of the state but is perpetrated by men whom women know.[1] This landscape emerges from a long history of state-sanctioned rape of women of color, before and after the legal institution of slavery, with total impunity. The institutionalized rape of women of color at the hands of the state has not been eliminated; it has only changed form (Collins 2004). As Andrea Ritchie details, "Far from being mere echoes of a distant past, the historical context of state violence against women and gender-nonconforming people of color in the United States deeply informs present-day interactions" (2017, 41).

In recent years, the systemic racism and historical silencing and erasure of women of color specifically in relation to efforts to name and resist sexual domination have also, and once again, surfaced. The Me Too movement, for all its feminist efforts to carve out an epistemic space to hear women's experiences with rape, has also minimized its legacy as a movement that began with a woman of color activist, Tarana Burke. The mainstream Me Too movement thus operates to obscure the experiences of women of color; in so doing, it enacts a historical appropriation and erasure of the activism and resistance of women of color to racialized heteropatriarchal domination. This racial structuring of the Me Too movement speaks to the inheritance of an epistemology and ontology of colonial difference in relation to gender. It draws attention to the fact that when white women speak about sexual domination, it becomes worthy of attention; their speech is granted a space for recognition (even if a marginal one). On my reading, this space is conferred because white women are legible as women. The contemporary racial politics of the Me Too movement are thus deeply related to Holtzclaw's framing of black women as the racialized other and signals the inheritance of colonial racist sexual domination far beyond the actions of Holtzclaw.

In this chapter, I make sense of how the racial politics of Me Too and the actions of Holtzclaw disclose how processes of racialization structure the subject position "woman" in the United States today. More specifically,

I draw attention to the way sexualized racism is deployed against women of color through a racial prohibition on woman that not only promotes sexual violence against women of color, as exemplified by Holtzclaw, but also encrusts colonial racism in the lived experience of becoming a woman, such that women of color remain in many ways unintelligible as women. The illegibility undermines their epistemic authority, bodily integrity, and dignity. I account for the historical formation and contemporary structure of racialized gender commitments and construction of woman as a racialized citizen-subject position that legitimizes and sanctions state violence against women of color.

I use the term "women of color" to refer to a diverse group of women of various racial, ethnic, and national backgrounds, knowing that it runs the risk of conceptually homogenizing such women. I also know this risk is potentially amplified by my own racial positioning as white. I also do not speak about the particular and different ways state-sanctioned rape has been and is perpetrated against women of color depending on their race, ethnicity, national origin, or gender presentation. For instance, while the experience of border rape is an experience of state-sanctioned rape unique to the immigrant women at the U.S.–Mexico border (Falcón 2001), Native and American Indian women often endure rape under the constraint of sexual slavery produced by the material effects of forced relocation (Deer 2015), and African American women are routinely violated in illegal strip and cavity searches (Ritchie 2017). Moreover, police rape against trans women of color has its own history and particular way of materializing in ways that resonate with, but also differ from, the ways cis women of color are victimized (Mogul, Ritchie, and Whitlock 2011; Stanley, Smith, and McDonald 2015; Ritchie 2017). I acknowledge that I do not talk about the specificity of the arsenal of rape that the state deploys against women of color, and I do not discuss the dynamic and multiple forms of resistance by women of color to police violence. Nevertheless, by centering the phenomenon of state-sanctioned rape against women of color and drawing on women of color feminisms, I hope to show how gender and feminine existence in particular are normatively constructed through and in order to maintain this reality.

Whereas in the previous chapter I discuss the relation between becoming a feminine existence—that is, becoming a woman in the racialized heteropatriarchal mode—and temporality, namely how such an existence is structured by a particular relation to time, here I account for the way colonial racism and its temporal structures underlie and inflect this construction. In particular, I consider how sexual domination is differentially deployed against women of color to produce and maintain feminine existence as a particularly white operation of gender. Thus, this chapter examines how racialized temporalities and racist colonial legacies of sexual domination are deep, underlying structures of feminine existence. To do so, I turn to discussions of the coloniality of gender and time. In my view, a consideration of the way time is racialized—the way time, as black feminist theorist Brittney Cooper (2016) says, is owned by white people—elucidates the way racialized temporality structures both gender as a social category and the normative experience of woman, that is, feminine existence, and is a justificatory apparatus of state violence against women of color. Contemporary normative gender formations inherit colonial racism and state violence against women of color through the racialization of time, which means that normative genders are lived and undertaken in the service of racialized gendered state violence that is always sexualized.

I argue that a racialized, colonial structure of linear temporality is keyed into feminine existence through the conceptual apparatus of a colonial sex/gender system, a system that is materially instituted through historical deployments of sexualized colonial conquest. The contemporary racism endured by women of color is therefore one that is deeply sexualized. Although "gendered racism" is the more prevalent term to name the experience or intertwining of multiple forms of oppression, namely sexism and racism, endured specifically by women of color (Essed 1991), here I use the term "sexualized racism" to underscore how the confluence of colonial temporality and processes of heterosexism and deployments of rape are inherently an operation of sexualized dehumanization that denies human status to women of color by denying them gender. As a white scholar, I acknowledge that my use of "sexualized racism" instead of "gendered racism" potentially undermines the epistemic authority of women of color regarding their oppression. I am, however, not denying the reality of gendered racism. Instead, I am striving to account for the depth of colonial ideologies and processes of sexual domination in such racism that may otherwise be obscured by the term itself.

I first draw attention to the way queer theorists account for the relation between heteronormative gender, linear temporality, and subject status. In the spirit of women of color feminisms and queer of color critique, I argue that a consideration of the way linearity is racialized is edifying.

Consequently, in the second section, drawing significantly on the work of María Lugones, I argue that normative gender formation is an effect of the colonial use of linear temporality, which is concretized through the historical use of rape against colonized women. In the last section, I consider the inheritance of the coloniality of gender and time in lived experience. I develop a preliminary phenomenological reading of racialized, gendered temporality in relation to contemporary state/police rape against women of color. I conclude by considering how feminine existence is a lived operation of what Lugones calls the light side of the colonial/modern gender system that is created by and sustains state-sanctioned violence against women of color.

Linear Time and Normative Gender

Many queer theorists have raised questions about how linear conceptions of time are used to constitute heteronormative subjects (Halberstam 2005; Freccero 2006; Dinshaw et al. 2007; Freeman 2010). Elizabeth Freeman's discussion of the production of "socially meaningful embodiment through temporal regulation" in *Time Binds* is perhaps one of the most impactful discussions about the role of temporality in heteronormative existence (2010, 3). For Freeman, there are particular structures, uses, and regulations of time that are mechanisms of social and existential constraint. She takes particular interest in the gendering of time through industrial wage work, the time line of heterosexual kinship, and the state's ordering of life through a temporal narrative that begins with a birth certificate and moves through a "sequence of socioeconomically 'productive' moments," including participating in formal wage labor that is coupled with marriage and reproduction (5). Freeman names this temporal ordering chrononormativity, which she takes to be a normative process that orients and regulates bodies and lives toward (heterosexual) reproduction through temporal regulation. As a normative process, chrononormativity constitutes and synchronizes individual lives to a collective social temporality. Drawing on Dana Luciano's (2007) notion of chronobiopolitics, Freeman suggests that chrononormative temporality "extends beyond individual anatomies to encompass the management of entire populations. . . . In a chronobiological society, the state and other institutions including representational apparatuses, link properly temporalized bodies to narratives of movement and change" (2010, 4). On Freeman's account, this "proper" temporal binding of individuals to a state is achieved through teleological schemes or the progressive linear ordering of life.

In the United States, the achievement of an intelligible and humanizing gender subjectivity exemplifies the chronobiopolitics of gender. For instance, the reproductive technologies that mark the sex of a fetus, a sex assignment that is then officially marked on a birth certificate, and assumed in and justified through cultural, medical, and psychological narratives about gender, begins and frames the teleological time line of gendered citizen subjectivity (Spade 2003). The F or M on the birth certificate is bound to a trajectory of compulsory life events—ones that can be resisted and negotiated but that nonetheless are tied to the management of the nation's population. This birth mark of gender is also entangled with expectations of heteronormativity, which serves to reify and justify the birth mark as the truth of a subject (Butler [1990] 1999, 1993). The deep social and legal resistance to the efforts of trans activists and allies who challenge the alleged fixity of the birth certificate's designation is just one example of the nation's investment in teleological gender narratives and existence. The harm of such teleological schemes and narratives is not only that they are compulsory operations of a justified existence but also that they are how "historically specific regimes of asymmetrical power" become "ordinary body tempos and routines" (Freeman 2010, 3). The result of this temporal embodiment of systems of power is that to be intelligible to the state, one must embody its temporal legacies of oppression.

The temporal materialization of heteronormativity is a linear sense and embodiment of time bound to an organized and coherent unfolding of heterosexual reproduction and kinship. This notion of straight time can be understood in phenomenological terms as the temporal horizon of normative gender constitution. Or, to follow Sara Ahmed (2006), a linear and coherent enactment of time vis-à-vis normatively gendered heterosexuality and heterosexualized genders is a straightening device, a conferral of a heteronormative orientation or mode of inhabiting the world through a lived experience of time as linear. As such, not only is heteronormativity chrononormativity par excellence and thus a central operation of chronobiopolitics, but it is also, as temporality, a practically intangible embodiment as well as a social enforcement of homophobia and, I would argue, transphobia as gateways to citizenship status.

However, heteronormative ideals of American citizenship are profoundly racialized (Ferguson 2003, 2005). In the context of the United States, the constellation of historical and ideological constructions and practices of kinship and sexuality that create and solidify citizenship have always been entangled with white supremacy, white settler colonial deployments of state violence, and the racialized regulation of national borders and citizenship. Although the formation of citizen-subjects through the establishment of racial borders and racist geographies crosses and subordinates people of color in various ways, that the nation's subject position is constituted as white is certain. The construction and enforcement of citizenship through colonial racial difference is not only tied to straight time, however. Citizenship not only is enacted through a linear and coherent cisgender heterosexuality but also is tied to a Eurocentric sense of time as linear. As many decolonial, third world feminist, and black feminist thinkers convey, the racial project of white supremacy imposes and is structured by a temporal order that situates white people as "those who order the world" and as those who "master time" (Holland 2012, 10). It is important, then, to consider how chrononormativity as a normative sexualized gendering of time is a process of racialization and a way of managing the race of a population; and it is important to consider what historical and material practices create and solidify this management.[2]

In my view, the chrononorms of normative genders are indebted to the colonial construction of time as linear. As I argue below, the very construction of the concept of "gender" is a colonial arrangement achieved through and structured by a heterosexist racialization of time. Moreover, although the racist construction and reality of rape is a central concern in feminist thought, it is rarely considered in the context of queer theory as a regulatory mechanism of white heteronormativity. This particular use of rape is necessary to the operation and maintenance of colonial time and gender configurations.

The Coloniality of Gender and Time

One of the most important contributions to feminist philosophical thinking about the co-constitution of gender and race as a colonial process is Latina decolonial philosopher María Lugones's account of the colonial/modern gender system. For Lugones, the modern system of gender as a binary social classification and lived reality emerges out of and as a weapon of the concrete material practices and epistemology of colonial domination. Although Lugones does not take up questions of temporality, other decolonial and

Latin American thinkers do. Consequently, I bring Lugones's account of modern gender formation in conversation with discussions of colonial temporality in order to show how linear temporality is a central operation of the colonial racialization of gender as well as to underscore that the linear temporality elucidated and criticized in queer theory as normative temporality has its roots in colonial linearity.

Lugones's primary task in her work on gender is to situate contemporary gender formations within the historical and ideological context of colonial conquest and racial identity formation. She argues that a central structure of colonial power is a racialized sex/gender distinction, which reserves and confers gender onto white bodies and sex onto black bodies, therefore creating and reinforcing colonial racial difference. As forms of social classification, Lugones claims, gender humanizes the colonizers while sex dehumanizes the colonized. This racialized and hierarchical distinction between gender and sex is the base structure of what Lugones calls the colonial/modern gender system or the coloniality of gender.

Lugones develops her account of gender as a colonial racial formation through a feminist appropriation of Aníbal Quijano's notion of the coloniality of power. For Quijano (2000a, 2000b), the coloniality of power names a system of control and domination that emerges in relation to but is distinct from the historical events of European colonialism. The concept, Quijano argues, offers a way to articulate the integration and justification of colonial ideology and conquest into ways of thinking and being in the modern world. Central to the coloniality of power is the introduction of race as, for Quijano, the central hierarchical social classification, making race an epistemological and ontological framework that adjudicates human status and justifies the colonization of certain people and places. As such, the notion of race is wed to the construction of other epistemological dichotomies that confer and codify social status—white/black, colonizer/colonized, superior/inferior, human/nonhuman. This racialized distinction becomes justification for racist social relations and patterns of domination and subordination that exceed but are also entangled with explicit political or economic colonial conquest.

According to Lugones, and I would agree, Quijano does not pay critical attention to the role of gender in the production and maintenance of the coloniality of power. In fact, Lugones argues that Quijano "accepts the global, Eurocentered, capitalist understanding of what gender is about" and therefore fails to consider how notions of gender emerge within and are instrumental to the operation of coloniality (2007, 189). Quijano's account, Lugones claims, overlooks gender as a process of colonial racialization. In contrast, she argues that coloniality is in fact structured by new gender formations that constitute and are constituted by race: "Colonialism did not impose precolonial, European gender arrangements on the colonized. It imposed a new gender system that created very different arrangements for colonized males and females than for white bourgeois colonizers" (186).

For Lugones, the new gender system, what she terms the colonial/modern gender system, is established and structured by a racialized sex/gender distinction. She argues that the new gender system includes the institution of the particular gender categories of "man" and "woman" as civilizing categories that humanize and racialize bodies as white and human and thus as superior to colonized people. However, this racialization of gender requires the imposition and projection of a dimorphic notion of sex onto the colonized. Accordingly, in the colonial/modern gender system, the colonized are understood as female or male—categories that demarcate their nonhuman, animal, and uncivilized status. As Lugones puts it:

> Beginning with the colonization of the Americas and the Caribbean, a hierarchical, dichotomous distinction between human and non-human was imposed on the colonized in the service of Western man. It was accompanied by other dichotomous hierarchical distinctions, among them that between men and women. This distinction became a mark of the human and a mark of civilization. Only the civilized are men or women. Indigenous peoples of the Americas and enslaved Africans were classified as not human in species—as animals, uncontrollably sexual and wild. (2010, 743)

From this view, the marks of white gender and black sex generate and systemize colonial difference and make the category "women of color" a logical impossibility (742). The confluence of colonial and racial gender formations "(white) man" and "(white) woman" are the terms that adjudicate who counts as human. The coloniality of gender makes it such that "no women are colonized; no colonized females are women" (756). The coloniality of gender thus names how gender intelligibility is a racialized mark of one's intelligibility as human.[3]

As a result of the ontological distinction conferred through the colonial/ modern gender system, Lugones insists that sex and gender are conceptually and materially separate. More simply, if one is marked as sex—male or female—then one is not and cannot be a gender—a man or a woman. In contrast to feminist conceptions of the sex/gender distinction wherein sex is understood as the material resource for the culturally produced gender, Lugones's account holds that the colonial ontology and epistemology does not link sex to gender but rather bifurcates them along racial lines. To be a female, for instance, makes one not-woman and thus nonhuman. On this reading of the sex/gender distinction, gender is a humanizing mark achieved through a racial mark of sex as animalistic.

It is important to note that Lugones's reading of the sex/gender distinction is quite different from how white feminists have traditionally understood and utilized it. In white Anglo-American feminist scholarship, the early appropriation of the sex/gender distinction was an effort to construct a theoretical framework in order to make visible gender as a cultural product distinct from a biological fact of sex. This distinction made it possible to articulate the social and cultural production of woman as a mediation of the raw material of sex in order to denounce biological determinism. In spite of its intention to challenge the view that women's inferiority is natural, later critiques of the sex/gender distinction show that it winds up recapitulating essentialist views in its failure to question the naturalness of sex (Butler [1990] 1999, 1993; Fausto-Sterling 2000). Other critiques point out that the distinction reifies the Eurocentric dichotomy between nature and culture in its pairing of nature to sex and culture to gender (Haraway 1991). Yet when read in relation to Lugones's account of the colonial distinction between sex and gender, one can see that the white Anglo-American feminist distinction does not consider how white women are always already removed from sex in ways that women of color are not. For instance, Judith Butler's well-known critique of the sex/gender distinction—that sex is and has been gender all along—does not consider the way colonialism and race frame the distinction. My claim, following Lugones, is that the sex/gender distinction exists only insofar as it is a racialized one. In other words, sex may really be gender after all, but only if one is talking about what Lugones names the light side: the white side of the sex/gender system.

Accordingly, insofar as the coloniality of gender situates white women as protagonists in the Eurocentric story of civilization through the mark of gender, white women already occupied a denaturalized place among the world's population. White women have never simply been relegated to nature. Although the identification of women with nature (and in turn the identification of men to culture) is a central patriarchal theme and practice, Lugones's suggestion is that the modern colonial moment in which "woman" is instituted as a humanizing category is the same moment that whiteness is created. Thus, she sees the emergence of the modern woman and whiteness as one and the same. Distinct from those previously marked as women and viewed as nature, the newly intelligible modern woman emerges through and produces the modern racial hierarchy. Under coloniality, that is, white women become elevated from mere nature to the realm of the social; they become women who accompany the white man of reason. Those marked as black become intelligible as the material or nonhuman resource to be exploited and sexually (ab)used.

Although the white feminist distinction makes visible the cultural production of gender, it renders invisible the colonial production of the relationship between sex and gender, and therefore obscures the racialized material history of both social categories. The white feminist articulation of gender as cultural and sex as natural is thus the very same distinction made by the colonial/modern gender system as a way to conquer and control the colonized. Although whether or how precolonial non-Western, indigenous, and tribal gendered epistemologies and formations did exist is a contested and critical area of inquiry (Oyěwùmì 1997; Waters 2004; Deer 2015), as a conceptual framework, the colonial sex/gender distinction elucidates the racial structure of gender intelligibility, and in particular how the imposition of a racially exclusive conception of woman is constructed through a sexualized inferiorization of nonwhite females. In contrast to the dominant model of the relation between sex and gender, where to be female is to be woman, the racial separation between sex and gender means that female is inconsistent with woman.

However, as Lugones (2007) remarks, in the colonial imaginary, the colonized are paradoxically imagined to be at once dimorphic sex and as exceeding dimorphic sex. Because nonwhite people are understood to be animalistic, their very bodies, especially markers of sex like genitalia and breasts, are understood and imagined to be excessive, overly sexual, uncontrollable, and impure. The historical fetishization, exploitation, and commodification of nonwhite bodies—exhibited as freak shows, used in medical experiments, and more (e.g., Saartjie Baartman, Anarcha)—exemplifies the way colonized bodies are simultaneously marked as within and beyond binary sex. This historical mark of excessive sex, Lugones argues, makes sex radically separate from gender. Yet if the subordination of the colonized can occur through the mark of being excessively sexed, it is necessary to consider why the dimorphic model is needed in the first place. If sex and gender stand alone, as Lugones insists, then the colonized do not need to be both sexually dimorphic and excessive. They need only be considered an excess in order to be rendered nonhuman. To make sense of why sex doubly marks the colonized, I suggest sex and gender are distinct but also inextricably linked. In my view, the colonial conception of "(white) woman" is constitutively entangled and thus inseparable from the racist construction of "(black) female." Although the colonized paradoxically are and are not understood through dimorphic sex classifications, in order for (binary) gender to be a civilizing mechanism of coloniality, dimorphic sex must be negated—that is, one is a woman because she is not female, which is to say woman is not prehuman. My contention is that this constitutive negation is produced through a colonial ordering of time—a linear ordering that is a central structure of the coloniality of gender.

Although often neglectful of a critical discussion of gender, discussions of temporality in Latin American philosophy do offer invaluable insights into the way a colonial conception of time as linear racially orders existence. According to Quijano (2000b), the geopolitical landscape carved out by the institution of race imparts meaning on geography (and the people who inhabit it), which is in part secured through a new conception of time. These shifts in relations to space and time matter because they sediment and justify colonial ideology as a system and as a European sensibility. In particular, he argues that a past/future dichotomy underlies the colonized/colonizer, nonhuman/human distinctions, which in turn positions the colonizers as temporally superior and makes a relation to time, in particular a relation to the past, a form of dehumanization. This temporal dehumanization discloses the ontological violence of Eurocentric epistemology. Walter Mignolo further develops the account of the coloniality of time, suggesting that time functions "as a principle of order that increasingly subordinates places, relegating them [the colonized] to before or below from the perspective of the 'holders (of the doors) of time'" (2002, 67). The relegation of the colonized as prior to the future situates the colonized as fully in the past and thus temporally dislocated from humanity. This temporal separation is paradoxical, however. Although the colonial view makes a clear distinction between the uncivilized past and the civilized present, there is a constitutive relationship between them. The uncivilized past is the necessary antecedent to civilized time. The coloniality of time is thus a temporal ordering that relies on hierarchical inseparability between the uncivilized past and the civilized present and future. This temporal order is linear; people and places are situated in a time line, one that has epistemic and ontological significance.

For Mignolo, the advent of linear time is a key "colonizing device" (2011, 152). On his account, the colonial chronology of humanity and civilization is a central apparatus in creating the racialized colonial difference. "It was by means of the concept of time," Mignolo writes, "that cultural differences were classified according to their proximity to modernity or to tradition" (160). The coloniality of time thus actualizes a temporal horizon for conceiving of and perceiving people and places. It actualizes a particular temporal experience of existence, one that prioritizes an origin of the Eurocentric present from which all knowledge, existence, and ways of being in the world unfold (Vallega 2014; Ortega 2016).

Even as there are various historical and material relations of race globally and in the geopolitical terrain of the United States, the coloniality of time is an invaluable conceptual framework for explaining the way racialized subject positions are bound to Eurocentric notions of time. Insofar as it positions those who are not white in a past that is exterior to the progressive temporality of (white) civilization—that is, modernity—the coloniality of time is a mechanism through which racial difference is realized and lived. It is the temporal amputation of the humanity of the colonized. When read alongside Lugones's account of the coloniality of gender, it is possible to see how the colonial time line structures and manifests as the colonial sex/gender distinction. Indeed, the linear temporal ordering should be understood as that which organizes the racialized difference between sex and gender. The civilizing gender category "woman" is structured by a constitutive relation to an uncivilized female past. In the colonial schema, sex is the temporal antagonist anterior to gender, a temporal relation that draws attention to the constitutive inseparability of "(black) female" to "(white) woman." If "woman" is to mark the human, it must be done so through and against the specter of its uncivilized past. "Female" is the mark of a wild or prehuman past—a past that must be negated but that is nevertheless internal to the operation of woman. The linear ordering of sex and gender, as a racialization of time, thus constructs woman as ahead of, in a racist evolutionary sense, female. Thus, according to the developmental temporal logic of the colonial sex/gender distinction, a woman is the human progression of a female animal. But for woman to exist, the category must bear a negative relation to female, which means the imposition of dimorphic sex is a necessary racial operation of gender. This point suggests that "woman" is a normative category rendered white only through a binding rejection of the specter of sex as the past.[4] At the same time, the colonial relation between woman and female, constituted temporally, suggests that sex is the raw material out of which gender is constructed only if by sex one means colonized bodies—that is, off the backs of and in violation of women of color.

There is, however, a deep logic of exclusion at work in the temporal difference between "woman" and "female." Although the former classification requires the negation of the latter, those who are marked as female cannot become women. To maintain the relegation of the colonized to the past, the linear relation between sex and gender must be fissured; it must be impossible for the colonized to become human. The simultaneous mark of race and sex produces this constitutive impossibility for black females to be intelligible as women in the colonial gender schema. To conceive of the colonized as at once dimorphic sex and as excessively sexed is a central way to produce this impossibility. The racialization of sex is thus double. It is distinct from the white category of gender, and it is also bifurcated along racial lines. The coloniality of gender is not just a by-product of the coloniality of being and time, however. Rather, the coloniality of gender is central to the use of time as a colonizing device. The colonial/modern gender system is one of the deeply visceral ways colonial linearity is taken up and materializes in lived experience. This co-constitutive relation between the coloniality of gender and time underscores the historical character of gender, but it also suggests that colonial processes are woven into subjective experience through the very convergence of racialized gender and temporality. As a colonial gendering device, linear temporality actualizes "(white) woman" and "(white) man" such that in the colonial schema, it is a particular racialized relation to time that confers and solidifies one's position as a normative—that is, intelligible—gendered subject. To be marked as a (legible) gender is to be already situated on the colonial time line, to be temporally situated in such a way that one's existence is humanized.

Importantly, this humanization is not achieved through a mere discursive or conceptual mark of new colonial classifications. It is realized through the sexual (ab)use of colonized females. More specifically, the use of state-sanctioned rape has long played a central role in the institution and organization of the colonial/modern gender system. In her formative work, *Women, Race, and Class*, Angela Davis accounts for the making of the category of Black woman. "The slave system defined Black people as chattel," Davis writes. "Since women, no less than men, were viewed as profitable labor-units, they might as well have been genderless as far as the slaveholders were concerned. . . . Black women were practically anomalies" (1981, 5). Anticipating Lugones's claims, Davis suggests that the very existence of enslaved Black women was practically impossible insofar as the material conditions of slavery minimized any differences between enslaved women and men. The exception to the racialized gender neutrality of slavery is, Davis argues, the experience of rape that was central in enslaved Black women's existence: "But women suffered in different ways [than men] as well, for they were victims of sexual abuse and other barbarous treatment that could only be inflicted on women" (9). The gendered difference among slaves was thus realized and made through the use of sexual violence.

This point about the legibility of Black women through racialized colonial sexual violence extends far beyond Black slaves. Indeed, this practice of colonial gendering has long been imposed on nonwhite women, although in different ways and for different reasons. For instance, the systematic and persistent use of sexual violence against Native and American Indian women was not only a form of subjugation, of rendering Indian country colonial property; it also made Native and American Indian women intelligible as female in the colonial framework. Consequently, one of the many egregious ramifications of this colonial use of sexual violence is that it produces a gendered epistemology. The genocidal rape of Native and American Indian women imposed the coloniality of gender and race, whereby Native and American Indian women became intelligible as female, a prehuman material resource, the very stuff in which white settlers sow their seed. In effect, as Paula Gunn Allen points out, this gendering—its imposition and its naturalization—"has, more than any other factor, led to the high incidence of rape and abuse of Indian women by Indian men" (1986, 203).

For Lugones, this use of rape is the dark side of the colonial/modern gender, the sexually violent undercurrent that gives rise to the humanizing genders of coloniality. Colonial linearity is a vital operation of the dark side insofar as it produces and pardons the physically violent dehumanization of colonized subjects. However, the temporal difference between woman and female materializes in large part through racialized rape. Even though, as Lugones notes, white women are also marked by sexual violability in the colonial schema, because they are classified as human, their relation to man confers a hold on the future (though a future that is his). In contrast, the use of rape against colonized women simultaneously constructs such women as females and thus as in the past at the same time that their victimization is vindicated through colonial temporality. However, the material conditions of many colonial institutions and specific events of colonial violence demand, acknowledge, and put to use the reproductive futurity of the colonized such that being tethered to the past is also bound to the exploitation of a particular future. The American institution of slavery, for instance, perceived a particular mode of futurity to be central to female slaves—indeed, to be central to their value as commodities. That is, female slaves were valued because they could create future progeny and thus property for white slave owners. This futurity, however, is not only mired in the temporality of the mark of sex—that is, it is bound to the animal function of mere procreation—but is also a theft of the possibility of controlling one's own reproductivity futurity. It is a loss of one's own future by having one's future be put to use, a use that sediments the colonial time line. Relatedly, as Sarah Clark Miller points out in her discussion of genocidal rape in Darfur, the mass use of rape against women is a way to harm the collective future of an entire community. Because "women often function as a node of cultural reproduction, maintaining and transmitting traditions to future generations," diminishing the future for a community is often done through the sexual violation of the women of the community (2009, 513). As Miller states, "Genocidal rapists hijack the reproductive abilities of a group, aiming to redirect the group's bloodline via forced impregnation of women and girls or to damage the reproductive capacities of the women and girls of the group" (513). It is thus not that colonized females are not taken to be capable of a future but that their future must be destroyed, often through rape, in order to anchor them to the past and mark them as sexed.

This temporal demotion and mark of sex institutes and is the colonial difference between the categories of "white woman" and "black female." To be marked as the gender "woman" thus requires a particular relation to time that is realized through and historically requires the use of rape against women of color, a use which is itself justified through the ideology of colonial temporality. As such, the colonial use of rape can be understood as a temporal ordering device of gender, and temporality is a justificatory mechanism of colonial uses of rape, both of which structure normative gender formations. This structuring mediates who can inhabit the social categories; it also underlies the existences of those who inhabit them.

To Live and Die by Sex

In *The Erotic Life of Racism*, Sharon Patricia Holland asks a provocative question about the spatiotemporal structure of contemporary racism: "What happens when someone who exists in time meets someone who only occupies space?" (2012, 10). In the context of this analysis, Holland's question can be one way to ask: What happens when a white man meets a black female? What happens when a black female crosses the state? For Holland, the answer is that the spatial quasi-subject, perceived as an interruption, an affront to the temporal subject's world making, is first accused of being-in-the-way, is met with a demand to move, and is reprimanded if she does not oblige the being-in-time. That is, the black female must oblige the human because he is the one who keeps the gates of time. On Holland's account, in a racist milieu, the black subject is not a maker of time; she does not exist as a subject spread out over and living in dynamic tension with the past, present, and future. Rather, the black subject is spatial—not only relegated to the past but stuck there. The colonial temporal relegation turns into a spatial positioning.

Yet the colonized subject is not merely in the past. She is a past that is present—hence the importance of Holland's question: when the static past crosses the white present, what are the existential and material consequences? To answer this question concretely, Holland offers a brief phenomenological reckoning of her own experience being constituted as a spatial subject by a being-in-time, a white woman, in a Safeway parking lot. In a racist encounter, a white woman demands that Holland, who is sitting in her car with her friend's daughter listening to a Tupac Shakur song while mourning his death, move her car so the white woman can load her groceries into her car. Holland does not oblige the white woman's exact demands but instead remains in the car to give her space. When the white woman is done loading, Holland exits her car and proceeds to be accused of being ungrateful for a white woman who marched for black people. This moment, as Holland makes clear, is laden with existential significance. The white woman expected something from Holland; she was supposed to get out of the way. This violation of Holland's agency is fundamentally temporal. She was made and expected to assume a position in which her time in the parking lot was bound to the demands of the white woman. Although it is true that existence is always bound to the demands of others, what makes Holland's experience a violation is that the white woman treated Holland as a thing, as without a time of her own. As Holland describes it, her presence in that present was "yoked . . . to the needs and desires of [her] white female counterpart" (2012, 10).

Reminiscent of Frantz Fanon's account of the epidermal racial schema in *Black Skin, White Masks* (1967), Holland draws attention to the way racialized subjectification renders the black body not simply inferior, but nonexistent as a body-subject. For Holland (2012), the denial of being in time is a disintegration of the self, an imprisonment in space, and as such a denial of her own material needs and desires. She becomes, like her car, a mere thing to be moved because the meeting of the black subject and the white subject does not occur in the same temporal field.

The clash of the two temporal planes, one that is dynamic while the other halted, is the racial logic through which there is a constant endeavor to order time through the mastery of colonized bodies. In the moment she is constituted by the white woman for the white woman, Holland's present, her presence, and her future are as well. In a true gesture of white supremacy, the white woman masters and regulates Holland's time. The paradox in the effort to master time, however, is that "in constantly trying to align the world according to a particular ordering, it arrests time rather than attests to its futurity" (2012, 19). More specifically, although the white woman "wanted to order time for" Holland through a manipulation of her experience of the space of the parking lot, Holland's refusal to comply makes the white woman turn "back the clock" to a racist past (18). Thus, as Holland suggests, the white present and its futurity are utterly reliant on perpetuating and turning to the past. But this reification of the colonial temporal order still grants the power of time to the white subject, which results in demoting the historically colonized body to space through the denial of being in time.[5]

Holland's experience is not unique. One need only consider that in April 2018, five African American women had the police called on them for taking too long on a golf course, or that in July 2018, Oregon state representative Janelle Bynum, a black woman, had the cops called on her for spending too much time at houses in a neighborhood in the predominantly white Clackamas County. Or how in 2015 fifteen-year-old Dajerria Becton was assaulted and violently arrested by a white police officer for being at a pool party, or how the 2015 death of Sandra Bland began when she did not signal when moving across lanes of traffic, did not put out her cigarette, and refused to move out of her car at the commands of former Texas trooper Brian Encinia. These are just a few of a surplus of enforced, violent spatial restrictions placed on women of color in recent years (and certainly, if one were to consider the recent restrictions placed on men of color and the restrictions placed on men and women of color in the distant past, the quantity of examples would only grow). In each of these instances, like Holland, when a black subject crosses the white plane, something is done to her. These few examples testify to the way a white world enforces a spatial prohibition that maintains the colonial time line.

Sara Ahmed conceives of the normative violence of colonial processes in primarily spatial terms, namely as a racialized "straightening" mechanism or a way of keeping existence in a white line. On her account, whiteness is "a straight line," a "line from which the world unfolds" (2006, 121). I have argued that the colonial time line is the straightening mechanism, a temporal order that, as Holland (2012) shows, spatially constitutes colonized bodies. According to Ahmed, the consequence of this spatial constitution is restriction: "For bodies that are not extended by the skin of the social, bodily movement is not so easy. Such bodies are stopped, where the stopping is an action that creates its own impressions. Who are you? Why are you here? What are you doing?" (2006, 121). Whether or not verbalized, this questioning underlies a racist social fabric, framing the black body-subject as questionable from the start. To be questionable is to already be in the mode of an impoverished temporal existence; it is to have one's existence, one's being, put on trial. To be questionable is to suspend the unfolding of an open future in relation to the past and present.

In the lived experience of the coloniality of gender, being in question is the refusal of a humanizing gender. From this view, it is possible to make phenomenological sense of Lugones's claim: "To see non-white women is to exceed 'categorical' logic" (2010, 742). Although women of color do exist, the racialized temporality of their existence undercuts not only their intelligibility as women but also their body schema as women in a white world. That is, the bodily inheritance of the coloniality of time severs their claim to woman in the deepest sense of being imprisoned in, as Lugones suggests, sex. Holland's experience in the parking lot, although a seemingly desexualized encounter, is structured by the white woman's inability to perceive their common situation as women, which is an operation of Holland's unintelligibility as a woman in a racist milieu. In other words, Holland's gendered existence is marked by an impossibility through the line of race, which is also the mark of sex as deep pastness that functions as a temporal foreclosing of the white woman's recognition of Holland as embodying a shared situation. Thus, the colonial sex/gender distinction preempts solidarity between women of color and white women. This point is not meant to suggest that such solidarity is impossible, but it is to suggest that colonial temporality is a pervasive horizon of intersubjective experience, which makes the recognition of a black woman as female and thus not-woman a likely feature of racialized encounters.

Although there are many concrete manifestations of this encounter, it takes on a particularly brutal form in the (always) sexualized encounter between women of color and U.S. law enforcement. Consider the following account told by Ritchie in her extensive analysis of state-sanctioned rape against women of color:

> In March 2013, Kim Nguyen, a twenty-seven-year-old graduate student, had been out drinking with friends in Los Angeles's Koreatown, and was standing in a parking lot waiting for a ride home when Officers David Shin and Jin Oh pulled up and began questioning them. Eventually they arrested Kim, but neither of her companions, for public intoxication, handcuffed her, and put her in the patrol car. One officer stayed in the backseat with her and began forcefully groping her, pulling up her skirt, forcing her legs apart, and grabbing her chest. Then, suddenly, the door behind her opened as the officers sped through a green light. Nguyen was thrown to the pavement, and can be seen on video captured by a nearby surveillance camera lying on the street with the top of her dress pulled down, her skirt hiked up, and severe injuries to her head. (2017, 118)

What is particularly pertinent about this encounter is that Nguyen's companions were both men. Her experience of the parking lot, her experience of that space as she crosses the path of the state, embodied by two male police officers, is structured by the perception of her as a spatial subject along racialized gender lines. It is important to stress that the particularities of Nguyen's racial positioning as an Asian American woman in the colonial schema is not identical to that of other women of color. Yet some aspects of the sexual conquest of women of color under coloniality elide the particularities of racialization. My suggestion is that one of those aspects is the mark of sex and thus the loss of time. To be more specific, whereas Nguyen's companions are permitted to move on, are granted a future, it is her existence, as a questionable woman, that structures the encounter. She is the one that must be put in place and is thus constituted as the receptacle for the temporal projects of the two male officers. Although, as I will discuss in chapter 3, Nguyen's companions may, at some other moment, be put in question, that they are not in this instance underscores that a particular gendered schema is at play. What makes the coloniality of gender a particularly appropriate lens through which to read this encounter between Nguyen and the state is that it discloses the way gender frames her as sex from the start. The rape perpetrated against Nguyen is the heterosexist weapon through which, to borrow a phrase from Holland, the officers bring Nguyen up under them, quite literally, in order to maintain the colonial time line. Importantly, the perpetrators need not even be white men so long as they bear a uniform of coloniality and enact the power of the state. Marking her as sex is the very enactment that constructs and reifies the colonial gender order.

In contrast to the many women who are victimized by police officers in Koreatown, Nguyen had the material and social resources to seek justice, or some small sense of it. Other women, those undocumented or undereducated, never seek legal recourse. Many of them disappear, leaving the spatiotemporal plane altogether. I draw attention to Nguyen's case because it is a particularly apt example of the contemporary lived experience of the coloniality of gender and time as and through a system of racialized sexual domination. As a consequence of her sexed position, she is framed from the get-go as out of order, and the use of rape is a way to get her back in place. As Ritchie's work makes clear, Nguyen's experience is but a small notch in the bedpost of the aggressor. The ideological racialized gender positioning of cis and trans women of color in the colonial schema renders their presence in the present a disruption to the order of things.

In its contemporary manifestation, state-sanctioned rape simultaneously enforces and constructs normative gender formations as a way to maintain order. Embedded in the colonial time line, then, is the weapon of state-sanctioned rape as a racialized gendering process. A phenomeno-logical consideration of the structure of the racist encounter as a spatial-ization of temporality suggests that although not every racist encounter a woman of color endures entails rape, state-sanctioned rape is a logical consequence. To have one's existence spatialized, an effect of the relegation to the deep past, is to be reduced to a sexed receptacle. It is to live and perhaps die by the colonial mark of sex. That the mark of sex is also a tem-poral ordering is significant. That this mark confers a particular relation to time suggests that to be branded by sex is to take up time, to live time in a way that is itself a colonial process of racialization. This is not to say that one cannot resist this colonial temporal ordering, but it does suggest that as a structure of experience, the colonial temporal logic is a preemptive device that keeps existence in a straight, white line.

The "Light Side"

Oklahoma City district attorney Lori McConnell's closing statement in the Holtzclaw trial draws attention to the sexualized racialization of gender in a most explicit way. As McConnell reminds the jury, Holtzclaw chose his victims banking on the reality that, in the eyes of the state and the nation, these women are unintelligible as "soccer moms" or "CEOs." How-ever, the thirteen black women Holtzclaw chose to rape were arguably not intelligible as women at all. Rather, Holtzclaw chose to rape thirteen black women because in Oklahoma the racialized gendered epistemology makes them unbelievable as women. Perhaps that the jury found him guilty is testimony to the reality that some white people do actually see black women as women. Indeed, the jurors seem to recognize the violation of black women's humanity in this trial, and perhaps it even bears witness to an unhinging of the coloniality of gender—although it is important to re-member that the plight of black women at the hands of the state is not remedied by a single trial outcome. In fact, a consideration of how the jury was persuaded in part by an appropriation of the colonial sex/gender dis-tinction itself suggests that the very racist heterogender ideology that justi-fied Holtzclaw's predatory behavior is far bigger and deeper than this trial. McConnell deploys, I suspect unknowingly, the colonial distinction in order to render human the thirteen black women for the white jury. In order to see the black women as victims, McConnell makes clear that they are not (white) soccer moms. While this distinction is used to persuade the jury to punish Holtzclaw and to humanize black women, in which the latter seems to use the distinction to challenge the coloniality of gender for justice, the distinction discloses that coloniality underlies the state's gender system. Accordingly, one must ask: how is woman ordinarily lived through this distinction?

Lugones holds that, along with the brutally violent dark side of the colonial/modern gender system, the light side of the system "constructs gender and gender relations hegemonically, ordering only the lives of white bourgeois men and women and constituting the modern/colonial meaning of men and women" (2007, 206). The hegemonic ordering internal to the colonial gender formations is heterosexuality—the sexualized economic, social, and political domination of women by men. The light side, itself a racialized manifestation of sexual domination, organizes existence in profoundly personal and political ways. Although Lugones does not offer a phenomenology of the light side, Beauvoir's account can be read as a description of the material and existential conditions of the light side. Since she does not explicitly spell out the way feminine existence is constituted as a colonial legacy, such a reading of Beauvoir exceeds what she herself says. As discussed in chapter 1, for Beauvoir, to assume one's existence as a woman in a sexist situation is to inhabit a feminine existence, which renders a woman dependent on men and as a sexualized instrument in their world-making projects. To undertake a feminine mode of being in the world is to inhabit an existential aesthetic of sexualized passivity and submission. When read as a colonial gender formation, becoming a woman as a feminine existence is to inherit a colonial history wherein "woman" is constituted not merely through a racial prohibition but also through one that requires and authorizes violence against women of color. In other words, to take up a feminine existence is to inhabit a norm that is constructed by and reifies the colonial distinction between gender and sex, which is the same ideological distinction that frames and justifies state-sanctioned rape against women of color.

As I've mentioned previously, not all women assume a feminine existence. Many fail to comply. Many resist. Others have different social, economic, and political contexts that offer other paths for existence, for better or worse. But to consider feminine existence as a colonial inheritance suggests that becoming an unquestionable woman in a racist society is to assume a relation to gender and time as an extension of state-sanctioned violence against women of color. Even as there are various individual, communal, and political practices of resistance, normative genders are today no less white. The historically entrenched and socially habituated norms and violence of coloniality are inherited in legible genders, the ones approved and protected by the state. Thus, to inhabit the state's operation of woman, whether by passive acceptance, compliance, or unwilful ignorance, compels the legacy of the colonial project and reinstates the colonial time line—and hence the continued urgency of the feminist question of how to inhabit woman, how to become a woman if one wants to become one, in ways that undo colonial processes and violence.

Yet the way the coloniality of gender and time works through us is not limited to the sedimentation of state-sanctioned rape against women of color and the corresponding juridical and social adjudication of woman. As we will see, white myths about rape are a central mechanism in the heteronormative regime of colonial gender as a lived experience. As affective regulatory mechanisms of heterosexist genders, white myths about rape set up the conditions of possibility for becoming a woman.

3

Beware of Strangers!

White Rape Myths and Lived Gender

It was Tuesday, June 16, 2015, when Donald Trump announced his candidacy for president of the United States. From inside the walls of Trump Tower in New York City, Trump delivered a speech to a crowd of supporters—a speech that painted a dire picture of the United States as a battered nation and "as a dumping ground for everybody else's problem."[1] But Trump clarified very quickly that by "everybody" he only meant Mexico, and by "problem" he meant Mexicans, especially Mexican men. "When Mexico sends its people, they're not sending their best. They're not sending you," proclaims Trump. "They're sending people that have lots of problems, and they're bringing those problems with us. They're bringing drugs. They're bringing crime. They're rapists" (Lee 2015). Roughly sixteen months later, on October 19, 2016, in the third and final presidential debate, Trump once again refers to Mexicans as "rapists," but this time adds "bad hombres" (Rhodan 2016).

Trump's remarks share a disturbing similarity with white supremacist terrorist Dylan Roof's justifications for murder discussed at the beginning of this book, and they also continue a particular presidential legacy of supporting white supremacist heteropatriarchal ideology exemplified by President Woodrow Wilson's screening of the propagandist film *The Birth of a Nation*. Both Trump and Roof use the white construction of men of color as rapists—the very construction at the heart of the film, and one deployed throughout the history of the United States to justify violence against communities of color and maintain white supremacy. That Trump's statement about Mexican men uses the same ideology that motivates Roof's white supremacist terrorism is quite clear, but white ignorance and negligence obfuscate such recognition. What interests me about Trump's white lies about Mexican men is not merely that, like white terrorist Roof, they draw on white supremacist ideologies about men of color or white myths about rape, but that they create and sustain a white horizon through which gender is lived.

Angela Davis (1981) is perhaps the best-known contemporary philosopher to offer a philosophical analysis of the racist framing of black men as rapists and its relation to gendered racism and racist gender formations.[2] For Davis, the white construction of black men and other men of color as rapists of white women is a central narrative *that shapes and motivates* the lived experience of whites in the United States. Other scholars have shown how this myth applies to all men of color, such that Trump's comments are a particular manifestation of the general white myth—a myth that literally shapes American citizenship (Wells 1892; Du Bois [1919] 1983; Bederman 1996; Freedman 2015). This myth is also one that justifies legislation that harms and curbs the freedom of people of color, immigrants, and trans people, and that constitutes and structures embodiment. Ultimately, a particularly egregious mythopoetic epistemology and ontology of racialized gender follows from the myth. As philosopher George Yancy suggests, it constitutes the body-subjects of men of color as not only predatory but also as phantoms, a fissured subject position that functions to frighten and unnerve, and in doing so affectively constitutes the racist white subject. Framed by the myth of the black male rapist, the presence of men of color in the white present are constituted as looming rapists that configure "the white self vis-à-vis the nonwhite self" (2008, 24).

While feminist thinkers, from academics to activists and journalists, have had much to say about the persistence of the white myth of the black male rapist, surprisingly little has been said about its relation to another central American myth about rape: the myth of stranger rape. Feminist psychologists have often discussed the ways rape myths and the prevalence of the myth of stranger rape in particular frame individual behavior in relation to and knowledge about rape, but I have yet to see this literature consider the racialized dimensions of the myth of stranger rape. Feminist philosopher Talia Mae Bettcher is one of the few thinkers to explicitly suggest "the myth of the stranger rapist is connected to the myth of the Black rapist" (2006, 208). Sara Ahmed draws attention to the racialization of fear (2004) and the way the figure of the stranger and stranger danger discourse figures through colonial racism (2000), yet the specific intertwining of the fear of the stranger and the fear of rape needs to be accounted for. In this chapter, I reflect on and untangle the connection in order to show that although Trump's comments are, in the context of American history and out of the mouths of white subjects, simultaneously normal (and therefore unexceptional) and egregious, the myth of the black male rapist circulates in a subtler and perhaps more insidious way through the myth of stranger rape. I am interested in the ways that the myth of stranger rape circulates as the myth of the black male rapist, and how that circulation constitutes and shapes embodied experience as a central operation of the colonial gender system. That is, I am interested in how the racist myth of stranger rape registers somatically to actualize the lived experience of feminine existence, and white female subjectivity in particular.

In chapter 2, I discussed the way state-sanctioned rape against women of color is central to the sedimentation of woman as a white subject position in the normative heterogender schema in the United States. The historical legacy and inheritance of rape against women of color is thus, as I state at the end of chapter 2, a mechanism through which the heteronormative regime of colonial gender is sedimented into the life of the nation and the life of the individual. This colonial legacy of rape is only a part of the arsenal of sexual domination deployed to tether the regime to the present. White myths about rape that have their own colonial legacy, related to but distinct from the deployment of rape, are vital to the operation of feminine existence. The particular significance of the use of white myths is that they are affective mechanisms that psychically occupy and generate the embodied lives of those to whom they are told. The widespread and persistent circulation of white myths about rape is, like the use of rape against women of color, a colonial legacy and inheritance; but myths do different work. In contrast to state-sanctioned rape, which structures woman as a racialized subject position, white myths actualize the embodiment or corporeal style of feminine existence. As I will show, the prevalence of the myth of stranger rape suggests that normative gendered embodiment is a primary vehicle for the production and maintenance of racist ideology. Although I believe Trump's comments have a similar effect—that is, they also produce and maintain racist heteronormative gender—that those who believe, consciously or not, the myth of stranger rape are rarely perceived as racist in the way Trump is by his critics is significant. While many (white) women may not say what Trump says, they might live gender in ways that do.

The Myth of the Black Male Rapist

The myth of the black male rapist is the irrational belief that men of color are out to rape white women. Although often accounted for with explicit reference to men of the African diaspora, the myth has been used to frame and criminalize men from various marginalized racial and ethnic groups. Beyond its literal meaning, feminist scholars have shown that this myth intends to create a particular racist and heterosexist social order such that identifying this belief about men of color as irrational, although foundational to the myth, barely cracks the surface of what the myth says and does (Davis 1981; Bederman 1996; McWhorter 2009). From a feminist point of view, the artificial image of the rape of white women by men of color is central to the creation and maintenance of a racist social order in which white men construct and obtain material and symbolic power through claims to the criminal, savage, and hypersexual nature of men of color under the guise that these claims are ethical and just because they protect white women. The myth of the black male rapist exposes a fear of and an effort to suppress the autonomy of men and women of color; it is an effort to produce a docile white female subject; and it supports and celebrates white male supremacy. Ultimately the feminist reading of the myth suggests that it is a weapon of racist extermination and a disciplinary mechanism central to the creation of racialized gendered persons.

In spite of and because of its mythical character, this racist framing of rape became a significant and haunting image in American life and in antirape movements. As Davis famously claims, "In the history of the United States, the fraudulent rape charge stands out as one of the most formidable artifices invented by racism" (1981, 173). It is well known that at the turn of the twentieth century, the myth became a salient feature in the dominant white American social imaginary as a way to justify the lynching of black men and as a means to paradoxically enact and conceal white supremacist terrorism. At this time, the myth drew on racist ideologies and science that claimed men of color were hypersexual, dangerous, and violent savages in order to encourage a hysterical fear of black men as sexual predators. The racist imaginary combined with Victorian ideals about white women's sexuality made this construction of men of color for a white audience highly efficacious and digestible as a supposedly logical representation. Consequently, in the dominant social psyche and the inner worlds of many white Americans, men of color became synonymous with rapists and white women with victims.

This myth creates a particular epistemology of rape and gender. In turning men of color into rapists of white women, rape "is premised on violating whiteness" (Gordon 1997b, 81). This racialization of rape obfuscates the history of white men's use of rape against women of color and the reality of intraracial rape. As such, the myth of the black male rapist is a way of thinking and perceiving rape that is vital to the protection of rapists. When rape is understood through a racialized frame, perceptions about rape and experiences of rape are distorted. Historically, this misrepresentation of rape has also fueled the construction and experience of gender. In particular, the racialization of the gender formation "man" through the racialized image of the rapist constructs white cis masculinity as good, positioning white cis men as acceptable, normal, good men who protect white cis women and constructing white cis women as fragile, weak, vulnerable, and helpless. This racialized conception of gender, a conception that organizes the lived experience of gender through a normalized system of racialized heterosexist dominance, is a primary effect of the myth of the black male rapist. Ultimately the myth exemplifies the way normative genders are structured through white lies about rape. Sustaining these lies is necessary to the maintenance of a racialized, gendered social order.[3]

The Myth of Stranger Rape

Feminists often use the concept of rape myths to name and describe a variety of ideas about rape that produce an impoverished but productive epistemology of rape that obscures its reality. The myth of the black male rapist is just one of many rape myths. Another prevalent and widely discussed myth about rape is the myth of stranger rape. As Lynn Phillips points out in her study of young women, sexuality, and domination, warnings young women receive about rape from family, friends, and teachers "focus on danger from strangers," which, "coupled with the lack of apparent concern about danger from acquaintances, suggests that only particular men rape or abuse women, and that these men are distinct from the men with whom women share their everyday lives" (2000, 55). Most young women have long learned that rapists are "'crazy-looking' strangers" as opposed to "'normal-looking' men" (56). Phillips's research underscores that young women in the United States are most likely to perceive rapists as bad guys who lurk behind bushes at night or sneak up behind women in dark public spaces as a result of cautionary tales about stranger danger they receive as girls.

Although feminist scholars have emphasized for several decades now the mismatch between fears and understandings of rape and its reality, it is astonishing how persistent the myth of stranger rape is today. Indeed, in my own experience teaching young cisgender women on university campuses in the United States, it is quite evident that the myth of stranger rape is anchored deep within their psychic domains. In fact, the cisgender women in my classes are often confused when they learn that they've bought into a rape myth because it feels so right to them. But even beyond my own experience, one need only consider the booming market of self-defense key chains that are marketed to, bought for and by, and carried by many girls and women to understand the hold of the myth on the individual and social imaginary. The presence and prevalence of the key chains disclose the very way the fear of the stranger rapist demarcates the lives of girls and women.

Self-defense strategies can, however, function as a form of empowerment and feminist embodiment for girls and women (McCaughey 1997; Hollander 2004, 2014; Cahill 2009; Cahill and Hunt 2016). Accordingly, carrying a self-defense key chain, even if it misunderstands the reality of rape, may have emancipatory effects in girls and women's lives. For instance, a young woman might feel empowered to take a jog at night if she has her safety key chain in hand—an exercise of her agency and a form of resistance to the existential and bodily constraints of a rape culture. However, my concern here is not about what the key chain might do for her. I gather that because defense practices can be modes of empowerment it does not necessarily matter whether they get the reality of rape right. My concern is that the presence and prevalence of self-defense key chains also reveals the presence and power of the stranger danger message. In chapter 5, I will return to this phenomenon to consider the temporal operation of cautionary tales about bad-guy rapists in the daily lives of girls and women, but here I want to consider how this particular image of the rapist as a stranger is a pervasive myth about race and gender.

The myth of stranger rape is the most central myth in what feminist psychologists call the real rape script, a commonly cited story about how rape occurs (Ryan 2011). According to Roger Schank and Robert Abelson, "A script is a predetermined, stereotyped sequence of actions that defines a well-known situation" (1977, 41). It is an apparatus that allows individuals to interpret, understand, and act in the world, informing and shaping the content and affects that are experienced in a given context. As a cognitive model for perceiving and recognizing rape, the real rape script influences a person's perception of what counts as rape and how it is most likely to occur. In the real rape script, rape involves a sudden attack by a stranger, typically a crazed man, on an unsuspecting woman. The woman in the script is walking alone, is outside at night, is deeply terrified, and is brutalized during the rape. The perpetrator, a stranger who lurks around dark and bare places, is considered overly aggressive and utterly violent.

Although the real rape script is incongruent with the reality of rape, it is a salient feature of the way many individuals, especially cisgender girls and women, understand and fear rape. Constructed as "real" rape, mythical stranger rape leads girls and women not only to adopt false assumptions about where they are safe and where they are in danger, but also to adopt certain bodily habits and modes of comportment in relation to allegedly dangerous spaces, times of day, and violent men. The internalization and embodiment of a false epistemology of rape creates what Gill Valentine refers to as "a mismatch between the geography of violence and the geography of fear" (1992, 22). In places where girls and women "perceive themselves to be at risk they are constantly alert to their physical surroundings, listening for every rustle in the bushes or approach of footsteps" (Valentine 1989, 386). Moreover, because this mismatch obfuscates the actual spaces in which women are most likely to be raped, as Sharon Marcus shows, "rapes often succeed as a result of women's fears," suggesting that the myth of stranger rape is a condition for the possibility of rape (1992, 394). In other words, the existence of the real rape script limits the definition of rape in lived experience, thereby constraining the field of perception of what counts as rape and who counts as a rapist.

Although many feminist and critical race scholars note that the crazy stranger of the real rape script is often imagined to be a man of color (Gordon 1997b; Katz 2006; Yancy 2008), few discussions offer a critical account of the relationship between the myth of the black male rapist and the myth of stranger rape.[4] This is surprising given that the two allegedly distinct myths share much in common. Both myths construct the image of the rapist as a man who is pathological and different, and they also construct the image of the victim as a vulnerable woman who is physically attacked when she is out in public. It is my contention that the two myths are actually the same myth. The myth of the black male rapist successfully masquerades as the myth of stranger rape, which means that the cautionary tales young women receive about stranger danger are really tales about normative schemas of gender and race. To acknowledge that the myth of stranger rape is a cloaked version of the myth of the black male rapist underscores the centrality of white lies about rape in the contemporary production and experience of race, gender, and rape.

Roland Barthes's (1972) notion of myth as a type of ideological speech can help reveal the deep connection between the myth of the black male rapist and the myth of stranger rape. For Barthes, myths originate not in the nature of things but in a sociopolitical context and have an explicitly political function. Barthes sees myths as signification systems that deliver messages about actual historical values and attitudes, though in a highly disguised way. On his account, a myth is not a falsehood but rather a political distortion of reality. The success of a myth depends on its ability to mask its ideological character by emptying the specific historical and political content of the myth. In doing so—that is, in concealing the cultural production—myths produce and maintain a particular social or political order while masquerading as fact. The affective dimension of this masquerade is that myths produce a particular epistemology and lived experience of the sociopolitical phenomena they signify.

Barthes's understanding of myth reminds us that myths shroud explicit historical and political content in order to retain the ideological meaning and function of such content. This means that the myth of the black male rapist need not appear specifically or explicitly as the myth of the black male rapist in order for it to actually be that myth. In fact, for Barthes, a myth is at its best when it partially redacts its ideological motives. Concealing the explicit racism from the myth is therefore a central way to keep the racist myth alive. If Barthes is right, it is actually best for the myth of the black male rapist to take other shapes, to have different ways of circulating if it is to remain an affective and efficacious apparatus. Since the ideological intent is actually amplified through its partial concealment, extracting some of the racist imagery from the myth of the black male rapist encourages the sociohistorical sedimentation of the myth. The image of the stranger conceals the overtly racist dimension of the image of the black male rapist.

Stranger rape is predicated by the idea that rapists are markedly different than the men whom girls and women live among on an ordinary basis. It is usually suggested, and rightly so, that that image of the stranger rapist leaves people ignorant to the reality that the majority of rapists are not strangers; they are often family, friends, or acquaintances. But it is also necessary to remember that being marked as a stranger has long been bound to processes of racialization and histories of colonialism that mark people of color as different, as outsiders, as significantly marked by strangeness. As James Baldwin (1953) and Frantz Fanon (1967) show, the experience of being a black man in a white world is an experience of being the stranger. Indeed, in the white settler worldview, non-Western and non-white bodies are always already strange, backward, and uncanny. Being a stranger, then, has never simply been about being someone who is not a family member, friend, or lover.

Rather, one becomes recognizable as a stranger through an ideological process in which one is constituted as a subject by being hailed by others through racialized differentiation (Ahmed 2000). Being marked as a stranger has been a process of racializing bodies and thus of racializing perception—or, as Ahmed writes, "The recognition of strangers brings into play relations of social and political antagonism that *mark some others as stranger than other* others" (2000, 23). The mark is a social and historical practice that patterns a particular way of constructing and structuring race, in turn rendering some bodies and places as inferior and dangerous. The mark of the stranger is thus, from a phenomenological view, an instrument in the process of racialization, understood as "the historical and social process by which races are constructed, seen and, when internalized or epidermalized, lived" (Al-Saji 2013, 4). The mark, as a persistent historical and social process, constitutes a particular perceptual field that structures individual and social habits of perception—habits that are prereflective. For the phenomenologist, that such habits are prereflective does not mean they are merely unconscious; rather, it means that they provide a horizon through which a particular object or subject is engaged.[5] They are generative of a way of relating to, of being affected by, and engaging that which is perceived.

Given that existence relies on habit to make sense of the world, it is important to understand how racializing vision is distinct from other perceptual habits. In her phenomenological account of racializing vision, Alia Al-Saji (2014) suggests that the difference lies in the way racializing habit is a practically closed operation. Racialized bodies "cannot be seen otherwise" (138). This negative, overdetermined habit of perception means that racialized bodies fail to register in different ways, generating an "*inability to see otherwise*" (139). The effects are thus primarily affective; in failing to be otherwise, the racialized body is perceived as, and indeed already constituted as, the stranger.

The 2015 trial and conviction of white, cisgender, heterosexual, upper-middle-class Stanford university student athlete/rapist Brock Turner provides an interesting example from which to think about the salience of the stranger-rapist myth. In June 2015, Turner, meeting neither the deracialized stranger rapist myth nor the racialized stranger myth, was found guilty of three counts of felony sexual assault, which he committed in January of that year. In the context of the history of the myth of the black male rapist and my claim that it is still a prevalent way of perceiving rape, it is surprising that Turner was found guilty at all. If the present were to mirror the past, Turner would never have gone on trial. But systems of power and histories of subordination and domination do not endure only by mirroring what once was. Whereas the sentiments of Trump and Roof show that contemporary expressions of power can mirror the past, Turner's case shows that they also persist through modification of the past. In Turner's case, his conviction shows that rapists are not strangers, but his sentencing certainly shows that "real" rapists are. In a nation that incarcerates people of color at extraordinarily high rates with harsher sentences, it is notable that Turner's sentencing was predicated by the damaging effects it would have on his life, and that he was released from prison after just three months for "good behavior."[6] What Turner's sentence shows is that while he may have been convicted of rape, that he even appeared as or could appear as a real rapist in the eyes of the court, the state, and the mainstream public is highly questionable.

The historical legacy of the image of the stranger as black thus has phenomenological, epistemological, and political consequences. As a perceptual habit, the association of blackness with strangeness has long been and remains a means to produce and mark racial difference, which in turn structures the horizon of perception. Although I recognize that many marks of otherness can mark one as strange and that strangeness is bound to anxieties over immigration and to ideologies of xenophobia—and is thus related to a larger history of colonization—in the American context, men of color have long been marked as invasive and violent strangers in white civilization. They are often both represented and perceived as the stranger. This racializing vision of strangeness has always been intimately connected to the charge of rape. It is this reality of a visible racial difference that the myth of stranger rape and the real rape script feeds off. While the construction and valuation of this racial difference is concealed, the lived historical reality and perception of racial difference is smuggled into and becomes the content of the myth. The image of the stranger is thus always already racialized, but it appears seemingly neutral inasmuch as the racial difference is not an explicitly standout feature in the myth of stranger rape.

When young women are warned "about accepting rides with strangers and of men hiding in the bushes," when they are taught that dangerous men are "visibly identifiable as abnormal," they are receiving lessons about the myth of the black male rapist (Phillips 2000, 56, 57). These messages transform the black rapist into the bad guy, thereby emptying the myth of its explicit historicity and racism. The bad guy is now the dark figure who lurks during the dark of the day. As such, the rapist is still constructed as a dark man through the imagery of the night. This is to suggest that the racialization of the rapist is woven into these warnings about dangerous men. Here the light/dark dichotomy that frames the normal/stranger dichotomy in the myth of the black male rapist transforms into a day/night dichotomy. This means that the image of the stranger draws on a narrative field that is replete with racist ideals and stereotypes. The black male rapist no longer needs to be the black male rapist because "stranger" is an adequate reference.

I gather that there may be instances in which the stranger danger discourse is helpful and preventative, and even unattached to racist epistemologies. But to overlook how the stranger is historically bound to modern processes of racialization and white supremacist myths about rape is to obscure the political function and ideological underpinnings of, as well as the racialized history of, stranger danger paranoia. Thus, when girls, especially white girls,[7] are taught to and in turn come to fear the man behind the bushes, their fear is largely predicated by a racialized conception of a rapist. That the myth structures their inner lives and the affective dimension of their existence means that although they don't say men of color are rapists, their fears certainly do.

White Myths and Feminine Existence

Although in feminist scholarship rape myths are an underlying concern, such work rarely underscores the way they are embodied as gendered projects. Here I want to suggest the need for a shift in the way feminists think about rape myths from that of mere epistemic deficiency and harm to a phenomenological consideration of embodied subjectivity. This shift opens up a way to understand the insidious persistence of rape myths and discloses how they constitute the experience of feminine existence. After all, if rape myths were merely false beliefs about rape, one would expect that it would be a rather simple task to clean up and sort out the epistemic field.

An analysis of the generative power of myth in embodied experience and collective unconscious is central to Beauvoir's analysis of feminine existence. In her detailed account of the myth of the Eternal Feminine, and its variations in theme—Woman as Mother, Woman as Nature, Woman as Goddess—Beauvoir is concerned with the justificatory operation of myth. For Beauvoir, the patriarchal myth of the Eternal Feminine simultaneously generates and mediates the possibilities of women's existence. It is the way a normative patriarchal conception of woman structures and is the vehicle through which gender is lived and embodied, turning the existential project of becoming into the destiny of being woman. From this view, Beauvoir advances an account of myth that suggests the existential function of myths is to impose a truth, or an essence, onto existence. As Debra Bergoffen claims in her reading of Beauvoir, "An essentializing structure, whether dignified as a metaphysical principle or unreflectively presumed in everyday life, is a myth. It prescribes the movement of becoming in order to contain it" (2002, 410).

In describing the particular contents and operation of the myth of the Eternal Feminine, Beauvoir shows how heteromasculinist mythology is one of the main systems of signification that allows men to deny their ontological ambiguity and justify the subordination of women (Scarth 2004); it also structures a woman's existence as a relative being. This dual operation means that the myth impoverishes women's material conditions and existential possibilities while simultaneously seducing women into embodying the myth. The myth of the Eternal Feminine permeates the inner worlds of men and women, ordering individual and collective ways of thinking, modes of desire, and embodied experience through patriarchal images and ideals of femininity. For Beauvoir, "the problem with the myth of femininity is that it directs women's desire to be toward an inessential being," and thus positions women as woman (Bergoffen 2002, 414). The myth actualizes the lived experience of a woman under the heteromasculinist image of woman. Following Bergoffen's reading of Beauvoir, it is possible to see that the myth of the Eternal Feminine is a primary way a woman's becoming is perverted into the essentialist structure of being woman.[8]

This is to say that the aesthetic or corporeal style of feminine existence is an effect of the embodiment of patriarchal mythology. Although not determinative of existence—there is the feminist possibility to fail at the myth—the patriarchal myth animates the embodied conditions of gender, turning the human condition of becoming into an almost essential gendered being. What is so powerful about this myth is that in the concrete situation in which it circulates, embodying the myth confers existential justification and recognition.

According to Beauvoir, then, patriarchal mythology is a mechanism through which normative gendered values and ideals are woven into subjectivity in ways that structure and actualize gendered existence. For many women, embodying the values and ideals of the myth of the Eternal Feminine is the only destiny offered to them; even for those whose field of possibility exceeds the myth, its justificatory operation nevertheless binds many women to it. In other words, the reason many women talk like, look like, move like, think like, and desire like woman is a result of the way the myth produces a limited and seemingly fixed field of recognition for the gendered subject position "woman." Importantly, the myth of the Eternal Feminine is laden with an ideology of sexual domination. The mythical image of woman is founded on erotic fantasies, metaphors, and values of conquest and sexualized obedience that render woman a natural essence and dangerous entity that must be tamed and dominated. This image of woman becomes for Beauvoir a constitutive ideological narrative underlying women's existence—a narrative that many women are often complicit with for the sake of justification and recognition.

Drawing on Beauvoir's account of patriarchal mythology, it is possible to understand that the function of rape mythology has never been to only create and circulate a false epistemology of rape. It has always been an affective mechanism through which individuals realize a gendered existence. The myth of the black male rapist has been a central historical force in the collective and individual actualization of feminine existence. Whereas Beauvoir shows how the myth of the Eternal Feminine offers (patriarchal) justification for a woman's existence, it is important to consider the way feminine existence is concretely entangled with white supremacist mythology because, in the United States in particular, the two mythologies are inextricably linked. More specifically, to embody the mythical image of the white woman in the myth—that is, to assume the style of the mythical white woman—is to realize the corporeal style of feminine existence. But whereas the myth of the Eternal Feminine works through desire (a desire to be), the myth of the black male rapist does its constitutive work through fear. To fear becoming a victim turns a woman into a relative being.

Ann Cahill's phenomenology of the fear of rape comes close to exposing the constitutive relation between patriarchal rape mythology and feminine existence. For Cahill, building on Young's account of female body comportment, feminine habits—habits that restrict and limit the space within which a woman's body can and does move—are an effect of girls' and women's experience of the fear that they could be raped. The power of the fear is not only that girls and women limit and restrict "their movement for safety's sake," but also that they inhabit their own bodies as fragile, weak, violable, and incapable of taking up space (Cahill 2001, 159). This experience of the body as a feminine body-subject is the experience of oneself as a previctim: "It produces and presents women as pre-victims expecting to be victimized" (159). While Cahill's account of the constitutive relation between the lived experience of the fear of rape and that of feminine existence is compelling, given the prevalence of the myth of the stranger rapist, it is important to consider how it produces and anchors the experience of the fear. While girls and women can and are raped in various places and are certainly subjected to public sexual harassment, that girls and women restrict their movements in space is generated by an assumption and feeling that certain spaces, and the wrong spaces in fact, are less safe. As I will discuss at length in chapter 5, given the prevalence of rape and the ideology of rape culture, it makes sense that girls and women fear rape; their lives are circumscribed by a haunting of rape. But if the lived experience of the fear matched the reality of rape, then the limited spaces in which girls and women often feel safe, for example the home, should actually be the ones they fear. A consideration of the way the experience of fear is racialized helps make sense of why girls and women restrict and limit their movement in public spaces as well as the times of day in which they move and constrict their bodies in public spaces. An account of the fear as racialized underscores the way the lived experience of the myth of the black male rapist realizes a feminine existence.

George Yancy's phenomenology of his experience as a man of color entering an elevator with a white woman underscores the way the myth of the black male rapist is central to the social production of and individual habituation to feminine existence:

I walk into the elevator and she feels apprehension. Her body shifts nervously and her heart beats more quickly as she clutches her purse more closely to her. She feels anxiety in the pit of her stomach. Her perception of time in the elevator may feel like an eternity. The space within the elevator is surrounded from all sides with my Black presence. . . . Her palms become clammy. She feels herself on the precipice of taking flight, the desperation to flee. There is panic, there is difficulty swallowing, and there is a slight trembling of her white torso, dry mouth, nausea. (2008, 5)

The white woman's bodily repertoire, as Yancy calls it, is the sedimentation of the myth. She fears Yancy not because he is a man but because he is a black man, a stranger. While the white woman may not even take herself to be racist, and while she may not even understand her fear, her racist fear is a gesture of her living body. Her body responds physiologically to the racist historical construct of the black man, actualizing a racialized gendered style of subjectivity. In her bodily comportment, the way she inhabits the space of her body in the space of the elevator she shares with a black man, she gesticulates racism: "Her racism involves habitual, somatically ingrained ways of whitely-being-in-the-world, and systematically racist institutional structures" that actualize racism as an "affective *embodied* response" (22–23). Her gestures—her panic, anxiety, trembling, and, one can imagine, a shrinking of her body in space as she moves as far away from Yancy and occupies only a sliver of the elevator as a form of protection—disclose the way historical narratives about race and rape, and in this case about black men in particular, are a prereflective or bodily knowing that are present in gestures of gender—that is, as a corporeal style.

What is especially significant about Yancy's account of the white woman in the elevator is that it shows how the woman constitutes her self as a feminine existence through the operation of the myth in her body. She is "not simply influenced by racist practices, but she is the *vehicle* through which such practices get performed and sustained" (2008, 22). Whereas Yancy is absolutely right to say that the white woman perceives a criminal black body that disrupts his existence as a body-subject, in doing so, the white woman also assumes and achieves a particular style of racialized gendered existence for herself. The white woman becomes the white woman of the mythical rape narrative who fears the black male rapist. I take it, as Yancy and others do, that the white woman on the elevator is not an exceptional white woman (see also Katz 2006). Rather, the very expression of her fear of him is indicative of the ways histories and systems of power are invested in and expressive gestures of the living body.

Yet what is alarming about the mutation of the overtly racist myth to its sanitized version is that the myth can seduce and actualize feminine existence even for women who are not white and even for white women who proclaim to be antiracist. If those who are or are perceived to be girls or women are taught and live out the myth of the stranger rapist, then the myth seduces women of various races and ethnicities into a feminine existence that is already racialized. As has been pointed out to me by several young women of color, it is not only white girls and women who buy into the myth of nonwhite male rapist. However, the difference in how a white woman lives out such an existence is that the myth is for her. She will be encouraged and even praised for her self-actualization through the myth. She will be able to accomplish herself as a feminine existence because it is a white existence. But that feminine existence is a conduit of racist practices does not necessarily mean that it is only a lived experience for white women. The confrontation with, embodied sedimentation of, or resistance to white myths and racist constructs of gender have as much to do with one's socioeconomic position, educational background, gender assignment at birth, and social, political, and religious affiliations. For instance, that most young women in university classrooms—women of various racial and ethnic backgrounds—live the fear of rape through the myth of stranger rape is not an indication of the universality or truth of the myth. Rather, it suggests that these women have a shared social horizon, whether it be class or educational background or national context. A shared social horizon structured by white supremacy certainly does not lead to a homogeneous existence for all women, but it at least offers a way to consider how, especially when inhabited in the absence of a critical consciousness or community, white myths inflect the existence of women of various backgrounds.

If the fear of rape is constructed by and thus filtered through white myths about rape, then rape myths are not just about erroneous cognition. They are affective mechanisms that sediment racist heterosexist practices, gestures, and histories in the living body. In doing so, they produce and mediate the lived experience of gender (and also rape). The myth of the black male rapist and its seemingly racially neutral twin has been and remains a central way a racist ideology is encrusted in and gesturally disclosed as feminine existence. The power of this rape myth in particular is that it sustains racist (hetero)sexual domination through the living body such that one need not say anything racist to actualize racism. Moreover, given that girls and women, especially white cis girls and women, are rewarded for assuming a feminine existence, they neither comprehend their own subordination even as they experience themselves as sexually violable nor comprehend their own complicity with and perpetuation of a racialized heteropatriarchy. This is not to say that girls and women have a false consciousness or are ignorant of their situations. Rather, it is to suggest that the ways one lives gender, one's gendered embodiment, may tacitly produce systems of domination in ways that elide conscious perception.

My point here is not to claim that women do not have any reason to fear the possibility of rape or stranger rape. Indeed, given the prevalence of rape by men against women, and given the pervasive atmosphere of misogyny and aggressive heterosexuality directed at women by men that characterizes a rape culture, it is unsurprising, even sensible, for girls and women to fear rape and to embody a gendered existence in ways that guard them from rape. I also do not want to deny that there is a constellation of forces at work in shaping the way girls and women perceive rape; I have only discussed one, albeit one that is a particularly significant inheritance of the past.

Moreover, it is also the case that stranger rape exists. According to the U.S. Bureau of Justice (2013), between 2005 and 2010, 22 percent of rapes were perpetrated by strangers, a percentage that has remained consistent since 1994. However, if all rapes were reported, this percentage would most likely be lower, especially because the rapes that are most likely to go unreported are those perpetrated by family, friends, lovers, and acquaintances—that is, anyone who is not a stranger. I do not deny that the reality of rape is pervasive and complex, and that rape myths can be realized. But my point is that many girls and women live gender in the service of white supremacy because they've been taught to fear rape in ways that perpetuate racist ideologies about rape. These fears and ideologies are further validated and justified when stranger rapes do occur, even though they are less likely to happen. A key consequence is that girls and women enact and become complicit with systems of racialized sexual domination at the same time that they are also oppressed by them.

The Past as Present

On the evening of February 18, 1915, *The Birth of a Nation*, D. W. Griffith's film adaption of Thomas Dixon's 1905 novel *The Clansman*, was screened inside the White House. President Woodrow Wilson ambiguously commended the film, claiming it was "like writing history with lightning" (see Benbow 2010). The film, more white supremacist propaganda than history or entertainment, and a testimony to the racism of a nation, was a climactic expression of the white fascination with the mythical image of the black male rapist. Twenty years earlier, Ida B. Wells (1895) had penned "The Red Record," documenting the way the myth was a central justification in the lynching of black men and a way to limit the freedom of African Americans in the United States. Wilson's screening of the film speaks to the reality that Wells's exposure of the myth as myth had little effect on the (white) national imaginary. Indeed, the film was a big hit. It sparked a rise in membership in the Ku Klux Klan for decades to come.

Although the widespread circulation of the myth of the black male rapist as white propaganda seems to have reached its peak in the early twentieth century, this past remains profoundly present in and as gendered embodiment. Certainly its overt disclosure exists, but this does not mean that only those who speak the myth in the most explicit form are racist. Historically, the affective power of the myth is undeniable. As a powerful mechanism of gendered racism and the production of racialized genders, its maintenance is crucial to white supremacist patriarchy. The affective power of the myth is one central way the normative gender of feminine existence has actualized, and continues to actualize. However, because the previctim of the myth is the white woman, the production of feminine existence as white female subjectivity remains an important conspirator in contemporary racism. As I will discuss in detail in chapter 5, what keeps the myth alive in the experience of becoming a woman is that the myth is spectral. Although it is a past that is present—that is, it is a history that is taken up in lived experience—it is nevertheless lived as a present absence.

The difference between the overt racism predicated on and perpetuating white rape mythology exemplified by Trump's remarks about Mexican and Mexican American men and the embodiment of such mythology by those who assume a feminine existence is a difference in degree, not kind. It may be comforting to believe that white supremacist patriarchal ideology vis-à-vis white rape mythology is enacted only by those who verbally espouse and overtly enact it, but my point throughout this chapter has been that such ideology structures (white) feminine subjectivity through the ways white rape mythology is taught to and circulates in girls' and women's lives. As a structure of experience, the ideology and mythology does not determine such experience; it is not a sufficient condition for assuming a feminine existence. However, historically, it is an existentially powerful one. The tacit allegiance to white men produced by an embodied commitment to white rape mythology offers one way to understand white women's continued support of white supremacist heteropatriarchy. At the same time, addressing the way white rape myths are generative of feminine existence, even in ways that may seduce girls and women of all racial and ethnic groups, underscores the way normative gendered subjectivity is entangled with racist histories and ideologies of sexual domination.

Ultimately white myths about rape conjured up in the past are not frozen in time. They persist through the experience of normative gender. That such myths are neither visible as myths nor legible as constitutive of gendered subjectivity is an effect of the temporality of gender. That it remains difficult for many individuals to grasp how their own experience of gender is entangled with historical constructs of heterosexism and racism is a result of gender as a profoundly personal habit. It is thus important to consider not just the temporality of feminine existence but also how feminine existence, as a particular style and experience of gender, actualizes in a way that obscures its social production.

Part II

The Present

The past is ever present. Contemporary ideas about race, gender, and sexuality did not drop from the sky.

—Patricia Hill Collins, *Black Sexual Politics*

4

Anonymity and the Temporality of Normative Gender

In this chapter, I offer a phenomenological account of gender normativity in order to examine the way social and historical constructs of racialized sexual domination engender the subject. The view of gender as a social construction is a paradigm of contemporary feminist thought, yet it has its limits. While the social constructionist view can account for the production of gender as it is external to the subject—that is, as gender is produced through historical events, economic systems, and social relations—it is less helpful in accounting for how those constructs are primarily lived in and as embodiment itself. Thus, whereas in the previous two chapters I have underscored the way historical systems of power and their ideological constructs produce and constrain the field of normative gender, in this chapter I embrace the phenomenological turn in feminist philosophy and give attention to the lived experience of these sociohistorical forces. Although feminist appropriations of Foucault and psychoanalysis have been fruitful resources for addressing the productive relationship between ideology, embodiment, and psychic life, that is, for how the external values and norms of the social world get inside the subject (Bartky 1990; Cornell 1995; Gatens 1995; Butler 1997), a phenomenology of the temporality of gender normativity elucidates the way social and historical constructs become the body-subject. In particular, this chapter draws attention to the actualization of normative gender through an embodied past, showing in turn that feminine existence materializes in and as bodily subjectivity through a past that renders its normative and constructed dimension invisible. By highlighting this temporal character of feminine existence, my aim is to show how constructs are temporally constituted as anonymous and thus primarily lived as a naturalized and abiding gendered self.

Feminist philosopher Linda Martín Alcoff argues that the truth of one's gender and racial identity is thought to be and "defined as that which can be seen" (2005, 7). This alleged and compulsory visibility to gender and racial identity is central to the structuring of social life and institutional processes. As Alcoff writes, "There is a visual registry operating in social relations that is socially constructed, historically evolving, and culturally variegated but nonetheless powerfully determinant over individual experience" (194). That gender and race are taken to be visible identities does not, of course, mean that they essentially or always operate as such. Indeed, ambiguous gender and racial identities are subjected to scrutiny and harm precisely because their visibility exceeds the visual registry that structures the dominant milieu. In one sense, Alcoff's account draws attention to the way visibility operates as a compulsory perceptual structure of dominant notions and experiences of gender and racial identity. In another, her aim is to make identities more visible, suggesting that it is not visibility itself that is the problem but rather the way visibility operates to hide the very operation and generation of gender and race. This chapter is partly motivated by Alcoff's question of the relation between visibility and identity. Here I suggest there is a necessary invisibility to the visibility of normative gender identity. There is a central paradox to normative gender: the visibility or presence of normative gender is often taken as a given—that I *just* am a woman or that all those around me are *just* men and women—such that the very generation of the visibility, the presence of normative gender, is rendered invisible. Thus, while I agree with Alcoff that gender and racial identities are thought to be and most often are lived through a structure of visibility, when it comes to normative gender, at the heart of this visibility is an invisibility that is central to maintaining the dominant order.

I draw attention to the anonymous temporality of normative gender to advance this view. One of my aims here is to understand not how normative gender becomes visible but how this very visibility is produced by an invisibility that is temporal in character. This temporal invisibility is a central way that the oppressive temporalities that structure feminine existence—the temporality of waiting, colonial temporalities, and so on—come to be and remain integral structures of women's subjectivity.

Judith Butler already offers an account of the way a temporality of gender conceals its production. For Butler, it is repetition that both produces and conceals gender as a socially constructed performance. Yet it's not clear to me that repetition captures the temporal accrual of normative gender in the life of the subject. Although Butler does not refer to mere repetition in the production of the gendered subject, different language is needed to understand the temporal depth that is required to become a feminine existence. I shift the focus away from the language of repetition to a phenomenological notion of temporality I borrow from Merleau-Ponty: anonymity. The shift from repetition to anonymity underscores the way feminine existence becomes entrenched in subjective life through an accumulation of the past such that it constitutes what Butler calls an abiding gendered self.

My point here is not to simply reaffirm the key feminist insight that gender is a naturalized phenomenon. Rather, my aim is to address how the habit of normative gender in particular is, to borrow a phrase from Merleau-Ponty, "a past that has never been present" (2012, 252). Thus, the feminist account of anonymity that I advance here, building on Merleau-Ponty, shows that feminine existence is realized through a generative past. Insofar as feminine existence is the primary phenomenon of concern in this book, the account I offer is focused on an account of the temporal embodiment and actualization of heteronormative gender as a persisting gendered style of one's existence—that is, as an embodied habit. In this sense, I am not talking here about the more momentary impositions and experiences of feminine existence that one may endure on the basis of being perceived in a certain way. Rather, I am concerned with the way the lived experience of feminine existence as a normative gendered existence endures as an individual and collective existence. This concern stems from the Beauvoirian view that the normative constraint of feminine existence harms women in particular ways and the respective queer, decolonial, and trans feminist views that underscore how the perpetuation of normative gender forecloses the field of gender in ways that harm abject and racialized others. However, despite this focus on the embodied habit of feminine existence, I suspect that aspects of my account are also generalizable to the lived experience of gender, whether normative or not, though I do not make any such claims.

Importantly, although Butler occasionally affirms and adopts phenomenological notions and insights in her work, as I will detail in what follows, she is also critical of phenomenological notions of subjectivity and embodiment. Here, as in chapter 1, I respond to Butler's reading of phenomenology less as a critique and more as a way to stage a rapprochement between feminist poststructuralism and feminist phenomenology vis-à-vis a consideration of the temporality of gender.[1] A focus on temporality provides a way to recuperate phenomenology for a feminist conception of gender that shows affinities with the critical insights of Butler's view but that nevertheless elucidates the generation of a normatively gendered subject in a way that Butler's account cannot.[2] My point here is not to dismiss Butler's work. Indeed, in chapter 5 I will show that her understanding of the spectrality of gender regulation (a kind of temporality itself) offers a way to address the constitutive relation between fears of rape and feminine existence.

The Metaphysics of Presence

In "Performative Acts and Gender Constitution: An Essay in Phenomenology and Feminist Theory," Butler asks, "How useful is a phenomenological departure for a feminist description of gender?" (1988, 522). Raising this question to the works of Merleau-Ponty and Beauvoir in particular, her answer is skeptical: "On the surface it appears that phenomenology shares with feminist analysis a commitment to grounding theory in lived experience, and in revealing the way in which the world is produced through the constituting acts of subjective experience" (522). Under the surface, however, the phenomenological commitment to lived experience, Butler claims, remains bound to a pregiven, constituting subject. Butler's concern is that the notion of experience relies on an individualistic assumption about acts. In addition, Butler challenges the plausibility of the phenomenological conception of the subject, arguing that phenomenology fails to take seriously how it presumes the embodied subject, including its materiality, as pregiven.

She elaborates on these claims in *Gender Trouble* ([1990] 1999) and *Bodies That Matter* (1993), where she formulates her critique of the metaphysics of substance as a central specter of feminist conceptions of woman and corporeality, calling into question their essentialist foundations and universalizing tendencies (see also Butler 1988, 1995, 1997). More specifically, she challenges Beauvoir and Luce Irigaray for their respective "insistence upon the coherence and unity of the category of women," which means that woman is not a temporally constituted position ([1990] 1999, 19). Butler's suspicion is that both Beauvoir and Irigaray commit to a metaphysics of substance, a view that takes woman to be rooted in a pregiven, unchanging foundation of the sexed body. According to Butler, this metaphysics of substance affirms gender essentialism, positing a fixed ground for the emergence of the gendered subject, and in doing so also posits gender as atemporal.

Reading Butler's critique of the metaphysics of substance alongside Jacques Derrida's critique of the metaphysics of presence helps further address the temporal concern at stake in Butler's suspicions of phenomenology and the metaphysics of substance. Derrida argues that phenomenology remains bound up in the notion of indivisible self-presence, a self-presence that accords to the Now or the temporal and foundational immediacy of the present. He says, "In phenomenology, the idea of primordial presence and in general of 'beginning,' 'absolute beginning' or principium, always refers back to" the point of the Now (1973, 61–62). This self-presence is invoked in the phenomenological method and is the epistemological foundation on which phenomenological insights rest. For Derrida, "the privilege of the present has never been put into question. It could not have been. It is what is self-evident itself, and no thought in the form of presence seems possible outside its element" (1982, 32). Left unquestioned, the primacy of the present elides the way phenomena always exceed the present and how the self is never present to itself. Derrida thus argues that the privilege afforded to the present becomes a paradoxical atemporality; there is no time other than the present and no thinking beyond presence.

Accordingly, the body is for Butler what the present is for Derrida. Both the body and the present are taken as atemporal foundations, which reproduce classical dualisms and metaphysical commitments that allege absolute, essential truths, presume direct access to reality, which Butler and Derrida take to be impossibilities, and conceal ideological and normative ideals and values. As I discuss at length in chapter 1, Butler offers a conception of gender as "an identity tenuously constituted *in time*" in order to undermine the metaphysics of substance in feminist accounts of gender ([1990] 1999, 191). Her temporal account of gender not only insists that gender is a doing but also suggests that the maintenance of intelligible or heteronormative gender is that which relies on a fictitious atemporality. In Derridean terms, this is to say that heteronormative gender is produced as a presence that is always present. The consequence, Butler insists, is that gender takes on a static metaphysical status, foreclosing a conception of gender as temporal. Thus, central to her own conception of gender is an account of the constitutive relation between the past and the present, which in turn offers a critique of the metaphysics of presence.

In her performative theory of gender, Butler prioritizes an account of the relation between gender and repetition, or an account of gender as in time. As she writes in the 1999 preface to *Gender Trouble*, "Performativity is not a singular act, but a repetition and a ritual, which achieves its effects through its naturalization in the context of a body, understood, in part, as a culturally sustained temporal duration" ([1990] 1999, xv). But her notion of repetition also entails a claim that gender is realized over time. In this sense, her account of repetition makes two distinct temporal claims, a claim to repetition and a claim to the temporal accrual of repetition, even as Butler herself tends to favor the notion of gender in time. Nevertheless, her performative theory of gender also suggests that the repetition of gendered acts becomes sediment that congeals over time, such that the materialization of gender is a temporal process of sedimentation. This refers to the way the doing of gender collects weight to construct and anchor an intelligible gendered subject—a subject with a temporal continuity and persistence that is central to normative gender legibility. As Butler puts it, "A sedimentation of gender norms produces the peculiar phenomenon of a 'natural sex' or a 'real woman' or any number of prevalent and compelling social fictions, and this is a sedimentation over time that has produced a set of corporeal styles which, in reified form, appear as the natural configuration of bodies into sexes in a binary relation to one another" ([1990] 1999, 191). Sedimentation is not, however, a central notion in her work (it appears a mere three times in *Gender Trouble*). Yet on my reading, it is significant insofar as it names the depth-giving process of repetition. In order for repeated acts and cultural norms to carry any subjective weight— that is, in order for them to have ontological significance—they must accrue and congeal. On this reading, Butler's conception of the naturalization of gender through the sedimentation of repetitive acts also frames the performative character of gender in relation to the past. If the ritual character of normative gender performance is the process of sedimentation, then there is a necessary temporal depth or a deep past to the appearance and presence of a heteronormative gendered subject. Butler's performative theory of gender thus disrupts the metaphysics of substance and the primacy of the present through the claim that repetition accrues as sedimentation.

Accordingly, the conception of intelligible gender as an incessant doing underscores the productive role of the past in making present a seemingly fixed gendered self. The reification of intelligible gender—gendered subjects who are coherent and legible according to heteronormative constructs—is thus an effect of sedimentation. Although for Butler all stylizations of gendered embodiment are temporally constituted, her notion of sedimentation suggests that normatively gendered subjects are an effect of the layering of acts repeated incessantly such that they harden and thicken as deposit.[3] In contrast, subversive acts are ones that undermine and disrupt the cultural and subjective thickness of repeated norms; as Butler puts it, "The possibilities of gender transformation are to be found precisely in the arbitrary relation between such acts, in the possibility of a failure to repeat, a deformity, or a parodic repetition that exposes the phantasmic effect of abiding identity as a politically tenuous construction" ([1990] 1999, 192).

Butler's conception of sedimentation is helpful for thinking about the entrenchment of heteronormative gender in cultural and subjective life. There is much more to say about a feminist account of normative gender as sedimentation, however. While Butler's account offers an important way to understand and challenge the metaphysics of substance, more can be said about sedimentation as a temporality of subjectivity, especially with regard to the way heteronormative gender is lived as a taken-for-granted presence. A phenomenological account of sedimentation highlights the way a gendered I is the lived experience of an embodied habit. The importance of this phenomenological view is that it begins to open up a way to consider how feminine existence is a particular experience of the past in the present.

Sedimentation and Habit

Following Butler, one can consider sedimentation as a temporal phenomenon that highlights how collective and individual existence takes shape through the accrued repetition of social, historical, and individual practices, values, and events. This accrual forms a seemingly natural foundation of gender that is actually its constructed artifice. A phenomenological account of sedimentation in particular shows how constructs of gender are temporally dialed into the life of the subject. Rather than taking a Butlerian view of sedimentation, which refers to the way repeated acts congeal as a stable but constructed ground for subjectivity, Merleau-Ponty's notion of sedimentation underscores that it is a temporal intentionality. For Merleau-Ponty, sedimentation is a temporal phenomenon through which one comes to be a particular (gendered) I in a way that elides presence even as the particularity is undoubtedly present.

For Merleau-Ponty, sedimentation is understood as an embodied knowledge of the world and of one's self. There is sedimentation of life "when an attitude toward the world has been confirmed often enough, it becomes privileged for us" (2012, 466). Sediment is that which allows the world and my existence in it to be an immediate situation for me. It allows a subject to count on "acquired concepts and judgments" or ways of moving in the world, "just as we count upon things that are there and that are given as a whole" (131). In this sense, sedimentation is the accumulation of the past that allows for the institution of a world or experience without this past having to be explicitly relived. It is an activity that allows for expansion through an unconscious recruiting of a past. However, as contracted knowledge, sedimentation "is not an inert mass at the foundation of our consciousness" (131). Instead, "the acquired . . . is only truly acquired if it is taken up in a new movement" (132). Sedimentation is a thus a kind of intentionality whereby the present is offered a sense, a meaning, through the weight of the past.

An explicit discussion of sedimentation is, however, thinly distributed in *Phenomenology of Perception*. Instead, Merleau-Ponty captures the phenomenon of sedimentation indirectly in his discussion of the habit-body. For Merleau-Ponty, the living body, understood as "an expressive space" that allows one to go "toward the world," is composed of "two distinct layers, that of the habitual body and that of the actual body" (2012, 330, 84). The habitual body is an operative intentionality that allows the world and one's body to unfold or actualize in a familiar way. It is the repository or sedimentation of habitual experience that actualizes a particular body schema, a familiar expressiveness of the living body that concretizes a definite milieu. This is exemplified by Merleau-Ponty's often cited discussion of the phantom limb. When an amputee senses his amputated arm, it is not a pathological response but rather the response of his past being in the world—a past world that was lived with two arms. As Merleau-Ponty writes, "What refuses the mutilation or the deficiency in us is an I that is engaged in a certain physical and inter-human world" (83). This means that the experience of "a phantom limb is to remain open to all of the actions of which the arm alone is capable and to stay within the practical field that one had prior to the mutilation" (84). In other words, one cannot sever one's past just by severing an arm. I have limbs that extend out to the world, whether physical, emotional, or other, in order to have the world I have. Thus, when an amputee experiences the phantom limb, it is the incorporation of past bodily habits into his present existence. For this reason, "the problem of how I can feel endowed with a limb that I no longer have in fact comes down to knowing how the habitual body can act as a guarantee for the actual body" (84). The actual recruits habit such that the amputee still actualizes his present as if it were like his past.

It is not, however, just in exceptional cases like amputation that the habitual body can be acknowledged. Merleau-Ponty makes this clear in his discussion of the habit body of a typist, claiming, "The subject who learns to type literally incorporates the space of the keyboard into his bodily space" (146). Similar to the amputee, the typist holds knowledge in his hands. He can find the keys, like the amputee could find his severed arm, without looking to the keys or his fingers. It is the living body that understands how to type, and this understanding comes through a habitual effort of one's limbs extending out to the world, or to a keyboard more specifically. Edward Casey underscores the habitual body as a kind of memory where "path-finding operations" generate so that the world and one's existence gain familiarity and concreteness (2000, 136). The habituation to typing generates a particular typist, just as the habituation to a particular sport generates a particular athlete. Accordingly, typing becomes a corporeal style for the particular typist through the sedimentation of the act of typing. Sedimentation is thus the accumulation of "knowledge in our hands" (Merleau-Ponty 2012, 145). When sediment forms, it becomes generative of a particular style of being-in-the-world. That is, sediment generates habit, which generates a mode or style of existence.

Feminist phenomenologists Sara Heinämaa and Linda Fisher extend Merleau-Ponty's account of sedimentation and habit to gender.[4] For Heinämaa, following Merleau-Ponty, we see that the gendered body is best "understood as a system—or better as sedimentation—of values and meanings, created by former bodily acts: postures, gestures, and movements" (1997, 302). Similarly, for Fisher, "gender is bodily habitude" (2011, 107). For both Fisher and Heinämaa, the thickness of the past, which is sedimentation, allows the body to remember such that gendered embodiment is facilitated through a bodily memory of the habitual body. When sediment gathers, habits actualize and allow for the world and existence to unfold in a way that resonates with previous unfoldings. The sedimentation of a style of gender is thus disclosed in the habitual body. As Fisher puts it, gender is "the sedimentation—itself a temporal notion—of meaning and significance, attained and (re)enacted through bodily action and motility, in the form of the habitual body and embodied memory." Insofar as it is "the body that understands, that acquires and enacts meaning," it "is the body that remembers" gender (2011, 98).

While Heinämaa and Fisher begin to offer a phenomenological account of the relationship between gender, sedimentation, and habituation, an explicit consideration of sedimentation and habituation as temporal phenomena edifies the phenomenological account of the generation of the gendered subject. It is my view that sedimentation and habituation are effects of what Merleau-Ponty refers to as anonymity. For Merleau-Ponty, subjectivity is an affective bodily accrual of the past such that a subject is generated from a "past that has never been present" or a past that never will be present as presence (2012, 252).[5] Framing the phenomenological discussion of gender around the temporal notion of anonymity underscores the presence of, in Butlerian terms, an abiding gendered self as an accumulation of the past. This turn to anonymity is not incompatible with and indeed builds on a phenomenological account of gender as habit. But highlighting the temporal depth of normative gender formations like feminine existence underscores the role temporality plays in the naturalization and internalization of oppressive subjectivities. The notion of anonymity raises the questions: What kind of past is normative gendered life? How is feminine existence a lived experience that is paradoxically past and present? How does normative gender appear and disappear at the same time?

Anonymity and Feminine Existence

Feminist philosophers have often been critical of the notion of anonymity. For instance, Elizabeth Grosz (1994) claims it ignores sexual difference and the particularity of embodiment. Shannon Sullivan (2001) also insists that anonymity overlooks difference and posits a genderless body, an impossibility in a world shaped by gender. These critical views of anonymity are premised in the feminist commitment that a neglect or refusal to perceive difference, in particular to fail to perceive the difference gender makes in one's existence, is not only ontologically amiss but also a perpetuation of patriarchal uses of gender neutrality as a guise for power. Given the historical absence and refusal to take differences such as gender, race, and sexuality as existential and structural forces in our lives, I agree with the feminist move to consider how differences shape embodiment and existence, and I also find a healthy feminist suspicion of genderless concepts and claims to be a critical philosophical and political inquiry.[6] I am not, however, suspicious of Merleau-Ponty's notion of anonymity in this way. Anonymity points to the temporality of the habitual body. Indeed, when understood as a temporal notion, anonymity provides a way to account for the pastness of normative gender (see Burke 2013).

In *Phenomenology of Perception*, Merleau-Ponty advances a notion of anonymity as a generative past that shapes but that is invisible in the present. He refers to anonymity in several ways: the anonymous body, "the pre-personal," "the impersonal," "an original past," "natural time," "primordial silence," "pre-history," and "a past which has never been present" (2012, 86/216/363, 85/167, 252, 168, 190, 250/265, 252). This kind of past, Merleau-Ponty claims, lies at the heart of subjectivity. Anonymity is that "which . . . is taken for granted, and to which I entrust the care of keeping me alive" (2012, 86).

Understanding this relation between anonymity and the care of keeping me alive requires paying attention to the distinctions Merleau-Ponty makes between impersonal and personal time and the tacit cogito and cogito. He insists that "life is made up of two rhythms," two temporalities, and an "*almost* impersonal existence," which "appears around our personal existence" (2012, 86). He connects the cogito—the present me or I—to the personal temporality of the present presence. I am here and now. But for Merleau-Ponty, the transparency of the Cartesian cogito, namely that I can grasp me in all my presence, is an impossibility precisely because there is always a past that creates an opacity to the present. He names this opacity the tacit cogito; it is the impersonal existence that at once exceeds presence and realizes the present. The tacit cogito is impersonal inasmuch as it is not an aspect of me that I can grasp. Thus, it is impersonal not because it is neutral but because it is not a presence. In contrast to the temporality of the I, the temporality of this impersonal existence is a generative past that flows anonymously in the present. As such, it is a past that is present but that I cannot perceive. But even as and precisely because I cannot perceive this past, it inflects and generates the present me. Thus, Merleau-Ponty's concern is with "the world . . . not perfectly explicit in front of us" (2012, 215). He suggests that perception is informed by a history such that "sensation is a reconstitution, it presupposes in me the sedimentations of previous constitutions" (222–23).

While the impersonal character of anonymity decenters the authority of the self-presence of the Cartesian cogito, what is most important for my reading is that anonymity draws our attention to the temporal depth of the subject. As the temporal undercurrent of the present I, anonymity is the accumulation of a past that allows a particular I to be realized without conscious reflection. It is "the generative" time of the "divisions, of experience, of things, and ideas" that are my personal time (Al-Saji 2008, 48). What Merleau-Ponty's account of anonymity discloses about subjectivity is that the presence of a subject is bound to, indeed is generated by, a temporality that cannot be consciously perceived. It is that which precedes the very me of the present, but that I nonetheless require to be here and now as me. Without the anonymous well of the past that flows without reflection into the present, I could not easily show up in the world as me. This prereflective recruitment of the past allows the particularity of me to feel grounded in the world. Or, to put it another way, my present happens through a continuous temporal undercurrent that anchors me in the world without conscious reflection. Anonymity is thus the temporality that allows me to sense my world and find my place in it. Anonymity is the temporal movement of sedimentation that allows a particular me to be at home in the world.

Understanding anonymity as a generative past can be concretized by turning again to the phantom limb. The amputee senses a prior time wherein two limbs actualized his world. Perceiving the world with two arms is one's habitual experience of the world such that I continue to exist in the world as if two limbs were present, just as I had two limbs in my past. When read in this way, anonymity can be understood as the temporal sedimentation that actualizes habit memory, the unconscious or anonymous sensing of the world that allows one to make a claim in the world as a particular subject. As Casey's discussion of habit memory shows, habit "works most forcefully and thoroughly when, rather than dominating, it recedes from the clamor of the present" (2000,163). Insofar as subjectivity is to always some extent habitual, it thus needs a temporality that is not present as presence.

A feminist phenomenological turn to anonymity offers a way to understand how subjects embody ideological gendered temporalities in such a way that renders them central but invisible to the gendered I. That is, to understand gender as an anonymous habit draws attention to the way the habit of gender recedes from the present such that although the habit is present, it exceeds visibility as habit and thus recedes from presence. So although normative gender may be habit, it is not lived as habit; it is lived as me. A normatively gendered existence is often and paradoxically lived as a forgotten habit, and thus its social and historical production is rendered invisible. Accordingly, understanding feminine existence as an anonymous phenomenon begins to account for the way normative gender is experienced or lived not as a repeated cultural construct but as a prereflective part of the self that temporalizes the personal, gendered I. Even as habits are repeated, normative gender is never lived as repetition because its very repetition exceeds personal existence. At the same time, normative gender is not merely repeated over time. It is an accumulation of past events, actions, interactions, ideologies, and histories that actualizes a gendered self.

It is primarily the actualization of a continuous and coherent gendered existence, or what Butler would call intelligible gender, that is realized as anonymous habit. For Butler, intelligible genders are realized through a repetition that naturalizes and reifies their appearance. As I will discuss further in chapter 6, the temporality of repetition is thus central to the sedimentation and construction of a heteronormative gender subjectivity. However, when understood as anonymous rather than repetitive, it is possible to understand how normative gender actualizes an I that lives gender as deeply personal but yet almost impossible to perceive. Insofar as normative gendered existence originates in a past that I cannot recall—it is something that I already do, that I already am—it actualizes anonymously. Feminine existence is a past that is at once generative and elides direct perception.

Although feminine existence has long been a justificatory style of gendered existence in the social realm—that is, it is a norm—the enduring generation of personal time as a feminine existence relies on an imperceptible temporal reservoir. To put it another way, feminine existence relies on the operation of norms at a temporal level underlying conscious and social life. This sedimentation of a past generates what Beauvoir terms a "general arrangement" of possible relations (2010, 341). Accordingly, this accumulation of a generative past is one that actualizes habits of gendered existence or particular modes of perception and being-in-the-world. But what makes normative gendered habits specifically bound to the temporality of anonymity is that their lack of fluidity and malleable responsivity results not from mere temporal duration but from the way they accumulate. As a normative habit of gender, feminine existence is an efficacious and productive habit when it withdraws as a presence. It is the very withdrawal from the present that maintains and solidifies the norm in me.

Assuming a feminine existence is an active and passive process—a woman makes and is made the other—but the sedimentation of feminine existence as me is generally lived in a forgotten sense. For instance, although a woman in her personal time may assume a feminine existence and take herself to be a woman, although she may easily say, "I am a woman," and although she may, with comfort, comport herself in traditionally feminine ways, ordinarily she does not directly perceive her gendered existence as an accumulation of her past. Most likely she will not even name her gendered existence a habit. She will feel it as just a part of her. Thus, she will live her feminine existence as a habit she cannot recall. If a child is assigned female at birth, raised as a girl, accepts most of her girling, much of which entails lessons in bodily practices and ways of acting that pattern normative ideologies in her embodiment and psychic life, she will be an accumulation of these lessons and hence of embodied normativity. But she will forget these lessons as lessons. She will forget that these lessons became her habits. She will live them as if they have always been with her. This is not because she merely repeats them but because of the way her past is invisibly generative of her present self. While a woman will have actively pursued and undertaken the accrual of these ideologies, they flow into her present as a past that exceeds her conscious life.

In the context of this inquiry, such an accumulation specifically refers to the accrual of historical constructs of racism and (hetero)sexual domination through experiences of time—experiences that in themselves often obscure the accumulation of a gendered life because temporality (as a structure of experience) and living histories (as horizons of experience) are generally imperceptible to the subject. When made habit, these histories are the sediment that materialize an abiding gendered self, a seemingly natural mode of being, which in actuality is an accumulation of a past with a particular ideological content. Thus, sexual domination and racial constructs of sexual domination become bodily habits generative of feminine existence, and as such they are invisibly entrenched into the experience of normative gender.

On this account, although normative gendered subjectivity like feminine existence is present and often hypervisible in the social realm, especially to those with feminist sensibilities, in the life of the subject it appears and disappears at the same time. It is simultaneously visible and invisible—a simultaneity that sustains the visibility of one's gender as just what is. This dis-appearance is a perceptual structure of normative gender because in order for it to appear as what has always been and will always be visible (socially and personally), its generative past must remain invisible. This point helps understand why, for instance, Alcoff (2005) aims to make gender and race more visible. It is an undoing of their paradoxical perceptual invisibility that exposes the operation of norms. Furthermore, understanding the anonymous sedimentation of feminine existence as a dis-appearance underscores why it is difficult to challenge and undo the hold of the norm on subjective life. What makes feminine existence so salient, so persistent, is that its very accrual as a particular past disappears. As rooted in me, normative gender is always a part of my I, my personal time, but as generated by anonymity, it is always prior to me, and hence I never perceive it for what it is. The trace of the habit and thus the past is effaced at the surface of the present such that normative gender is lived as if it has no past. It is lived as if it just is.

Importantly, the turn to anonymity that I have staged here also addresses Butler's critique of the phenomenological subject. There is no I who draws up the past to realize the present, but rather the past rushes through me in such a way that I do not constitute my gender; I am possessed by an anonymous past that realizes itself in me. Surging forth from anonymity to actualize the present, feminine existence is in the now and always elsewhere. There is a constitutive past at the heart of gendered subjectivity without which gender would make no gripping claim on existence. As anonymous, normative gendered existence "is a furrow that traces itself out magically under our eyes without a tracer, a certain hollow, a certain interior, a certain absence" (Merleau-Ponty 1968, 151).

Excess(ive) Gender?

Merleau-Ponty is clear that anonymity is not mere sedimentation such that it becomes determination.[7] Anonymity is not a unidirectional or singular temporality that generates a redundant and fixed subject. Instead, anonymity, as an embodied temporality that unfolds from the senses, exceeds static and singular subjectivity. It is characterized by plurality such that there is always a latent potential that past habits can be undone (see also Stoller 2011).

Gender, as feminist scholars have long argued, is not determined, essential, or eternal. It is, rather, excessive. Yet despite decades of thinking about the inherent instability to the normative, binary structure of gender, it's not so clear that the lived experience of gender has become significantly malleable. To be sure, the confines and regulations around socially acceptable gender presentations, aesthetics, and practices have shifted, but the force of the norm appears to be recalcitrant. So why, when gender is not actually fixed, does it appear to be? How does it come to be lived as if it were?

My response to these questions is that habits have a tight grip on existence. As Merleau-Ponty suggests, habits hold and anchor us not only in the world but in ourselves. But our gendered lives are not effects of mere repetition; they are effects of modification, of a movement of the past in the present that exceeds repetition. As Casey suggests, the coimmanence of habit—that habit is not just the influx of the past into the present—is what keeps them alive: "Instead of simply repeating this past [habit], it modifies it by extending intentional threads to ever-changing circumstances" (2000, 168). Thus, habits endure precisely as a past modified and transformed in the lived present. This point suggests that normative gendered existence is an accumulation of the past that, because it is not mere repetition, is difficult to interrupt. Insofar as habit is modified by the present and is thus rendered invisible as habit, the operation of the norm endures because it elides perception as a habitual act. My point here is not to suggest that living gender in excess of the norm is impossible, but it is to suggest that there is a certain obstinacy in the norm.

Importantly, this obstinacy is intensified by the very temporality of feminine existence. As a closed structure of temporality, the passive present preempts alteration; instead, similar to racialized habits, it "tends to be predictable and determinate in its effects" (Al-Saji 2014, 154). The temporality of feminine existence, which I detail at length in chapter 1, anchors a subject to a redundant present, and that very anchoring sediments the temporal habit by closing down possibilities. The endurance of feminine existence is, like all habits, a result of its ability to be modified, but its endurance is also an effect of its inability to be disrupted by other gendered habits. The temporality of feminine existence is a closed temporality and thus is difficult to fissure. It is a structure that aims to trap you and close you down. As a consequence, the temporality of feminine existence obstructs the plurality or excessive character of anonymity. Feminine existence is thus a difficult habit to undo because its very doing preempts change.

The way anonymity and the temporality of feminine existence work together to constrain possibility offers a way to understand the temporal difference between normative and subversive gendered existence. Although it is certainly the case that gendered habits that subvert, resist, queer, or destabilize normative gender subjectivity accrue as sediment and actualize a me and are thus anonymous, it is also the case that the generation of subversive gender requires a certain visibility. That visibility requires an exposure of the anonymous past. What makes a gendered existence that defies the operation of the norm distinct is that it confronts, in some way, that which has generated the constrained social and personal field of gendered existence and perception. Accordingly, in order to undo the grip of normative gender in one's life, one must come to grips with the grip itself. Coming to grips with normative gender requires opening up the perceptual field, which also means uncovering or excavating one's past of normative gender. In order to undermine the grip of feminine existence in particular, the accumulation of the past must be fractured. As I will detail in the last chapter of this book, in order for a feminine existence to become a feminist existence, the anonymous past must be drawn into the present as visible.

The anonymous persistence of normative gender also offers a way to understand how sexual domination is encrusted in the lived experience of gender. As I argued in the previous two chapters, legacies of racialized sexual domination are constitutive of and lived as an integral part of gendered life; more specifically, they are central to the operation and experience of feminine existence. They shape whom I become. Insofar as they structure existence, these living histories are taken up in the impersonal past, anonymously tethering sexual domination to feminine existence. As anonymous in the present, sexual domination can persist in the lived experience of feminine existence without being a presence. Indeed, it is this very capacity to elide presence that makes the present bound to legacies of sexual domination. The invisibility of sexual domination as a structuring process of feminine existence is another layer of the temporal constraint on gendered possibilities.

Yet it is still imperative to remember that although some habits are more difficult to change than others, all habits are indeterminate. Indeed, according to Merleau-Ponty, my I is never fully determined or purely singular because my anonymous life is an excess of sensations waiting to be actualized. Because the living body does not sense in the singular, I can actualize differently. So even though the actualization of feminine existence requires a thick and deep accumulation of the past in order to keep a grip on who one can become, it is the excessive dimension of ano-nymity that allows the hardened past to be disrupted and reconfigured. Gendered subjectivity can thus actualize in new and different ways because the past is excessive, pregnant with meaning and potential.

However, feminine existence is temporally constrained. This constraint overdetermines its actualization and undermines the plurality of anony-mous temporality. As will become clear in the next chapter, the temporal-ity of the normative threat of sexual domination is a pernicious specter of feminine existence that conspires to keep girls and women bound to it.

5

Specters of Violence

Feminist scholars have long accounted for the centrality of rape and the threat of rape in women's lives. From a feminist perspective, rape exemplifies men's power over women and defines a woman's existence as a woman; its prevalence keeps women in a constant state of fear (Brownmiller 1975; MacKinnon 1988, 1989, 2006).[1] As such, rape and its threat are a difference of degree, not kind; both operate as forms of sexual terrorism (Sheffield 1987). Feminist phenomenological analyses in particular have drawn attention to the way the centrality of the threat of rape structures women's experience, producing the feminine body and feminine existence (Young 1980; Cahill 2001). Many of them argue that feminine bodily habits are acquired and anchored into the subjective life of women from such a young age that girls and women understand and accept their bodies as endangered by or vulnerable to rape and other forms of sexual violation. This chapter expands on feminist accounts of the relationship between sexual violability and women's condition, affirming that the threat of rape is a central mechanism in the production of feminine existence. However, I expand on existing feminist scholarship by considering how the temporality of the threat of rape is central to the production and maintenance of feminine existence as a lived experience. The threat of rape is efficacious as a disciplinary force of gender subordination because of its temporal structure: spectrality.

Lynn M. Phillips's (2000) exploration of young women's experience of (hetero)sexuality and domination offers important insights into the relation between the spectrality of the threat and feminine existence. One of her interviewees, Andrea, a twenty-two-year-old mixed-race woman, offers one of the most explicit and provocative examples of this relation:

> I remember it was really scary, like you hear about these scary old perverts hiding in the bushes who leap out and abduct little girls. We were too young to know about the sexual stuff, but we knew something really awful could happen to little girls like us. So we

used to make up these scary stories, sort of like ghost stories, about these crazy-looking guys in trench coats with peg-legs or eye-patches who would steal little girls and kill them or something. We'd all get really scared, and then we'd laugh at each other for being scared, and then we'd tell another story. In a way, it was kind of a way of letting off steam, I guess, because I know we were all really scared. (56)

Andrea's testimony reveals the way the threat of rape operates as a haunting. Her reference to cautionary tales about rape as ghost stories suggests that the fear of rape is produced by the fact that it haunts existence. Whereas Andrea's use of ghost stories is a way to cope with the lurking possibility of rape, I want to draw attention to what is suggested about the operation of the threat of rape in the lives of girls and women through this narrative practice of ghost stories. In particular, by taking seriously the affective and disciplinary dimensions of ghosts, rape can be understood as a specter, a haunting, that is in part what makes one's existence a feminine one and what maintains one's experience of being a woman as tethered to assuming a feminine existence. Feminine existence is a gendered existence that is haunted by rape. Although it is certainly not the only gendered existence haunted by rape, the binding relation between this haunting and feminine existence is paramount to the maintenance of a rigid, exclusionary, and violent gender system.

I call this experience of the threat of rape in women's and girls' lives spectral violence because of the way it haunts, and in haunting organizes and terrorizes subjectivity and one's claim to freedom. As spectral violence, the normative threat of rape is a disciplinary mechanism that hurls a woman into a feminine existence. As I discuss in the introduction, feminine existence does not merely demarcate a feminine gender presentation or expression; it names a constrained mode of embodiment through which one is rendered passive, hailed as a split object-subject, and hurled into a misogynist ideology of woman.

By drawing attention to the relationship between spectral violence and feminine existence, I do not mean to reify or naturalize violence and rape in girls' and women's lives.[2] I gather that reimagining gender and possibilities of existence requires a turn away from constraint and violence. Yet I can't but help be preoccupied with the sustained role of rape and its threat in girls' and women's lives. Although much has changed since early feminist preoccupations, much has also stayed the same. My account of spectral violence offers a way to address why the present condition of women's existence looks and feels much like the past.

While theories of spectrality (Derrida 1994; Gordon 1997a; Brown 2001; Freccero 2007) have focused on the figure of the ghost as a demand, a haunting of the concealed past that, when made a presence, can open foreclosed possibility, I focus on the way specters work to regulate and constrain gender. Following Judith Butler's account of the specters of the abject, I draw attention to the way spectrality is an operation of gender maintenance. But unlike Butler's account of the specters of the abject, I do not understand the specter of rape to entail queer possibility. Indeed, a consideration of the threat of rape as a specter suggests what ghosts do in gendered life is not always the same and is not always the promise of liberatory disruption. Like other theories of spectrality, however, I focus on the temporality of the specter of rape in order to show how the productive effect of the normative threat is a result of its present absence—that is, a specter is a phenomenon that dis-appears. Importantly, this dis-appearance is distinct from the account of anonymity I advanced in chapter 4. In contrast to anonymity, which is a past that is present but not as presence, spectrality refers to the way the present is marked by an absence, by that which is not yet here, by that which may arrive in the future. Together, these two distinct accounts of temporalities of dis-appearance elucidate the way normative gender is lived, regulated, and enforced through paradoxically visible and invisible temporalities. Ultimately, to understand the threat of rape as a haunting is to address how sexual domination is a present absence that is central to limiting the possibilities of what it means to become a woman and to producing the material and existential conditions that impoverish the lives of girls and women.[3]

What is especially important about Andrea's ghost stories about rape is that they underscore the way the rape myths I discuss in chapter 3 operate psychically and temporally as a way to maintain the presence of feminine existence in our contemporary social world and embodied lives. My aim in part I of this book was to highlight key living histories that produce the field of gender and that structure feminine existence as a central possibility in this field. The history of colonial processes, including its mythical histories, becomes, as Andrea's experience makes clear, ghost stories that haunt individual existence. Their operation as ghosts, as specters, is related to and distinct from their operation as myths. As myths, they circulate a productive but false epistemology of rape and a productive epistemology of gender, both of which structure and produce gendered embodiment. This circulation as myth is necessary to the creation of, belief in, and felt experience of specters as real. But what the specters of rape do is unique. Although the ghost stories of rape I highlight in this book are not exhaustive, white histories and narratives about rape ghost existence in order to produce, constrain, and actualize a normative structure and lived experience of gender.

As I will discuss in what follows, distinct from the trauma of an experience of rape, the spectral violence that is the normative threat of rape has its own traumatic effects. These effects are lived by those who are haunted by the possibility of rape. A consideration of the spectrality of the normative threat thus begins to open up a consideration of the way violence and trauma mark girls and women who are not survivors of rape. That there is a trauma connection between potential and actual survivors does not undermine the difference or intensity of the trauma endured by survivors; rather, it highlights an insidious temporal barrier for survivors of rape to healing the wounds of rape's trauma.

Specters and Heterogender Subjectivity

Judith Butler's discussion of the specters of the abject in *Gender Trouble* ([1990] 1999) and *Bodies That Matter* (1993) is arguably the most influential consideration of the relation between specters, gender normativity, and subordination in feminist and queer scholarship. Most often, Butler refers to the specter of the abject as the constitutive outside or constraint that is actually inside of the hegemony of livable, heteronormative genders. The specter, however, is not a mere conceptual apparatus from which Butler makes a claim about gender intelligibility.[4] Rather, she argues that the specters are a densely populated realm of social life inhabited by queer bodies that, because they exceed the normative schema, render the binary heterogender norm vulnerable to exposure as fictitious. As a result of this queer excess and of the gender trouble it produces, the specters of the abject are excluded from the status of the subject—an exclusion that dehumanizes and renders the nonnormative as unintelligible and as unlivable. Ultimately, for Butler, the threat of the specter is that it can disrupt the normative schema of gender and expose its construction; this in turn opens up a can of emancipatory trouble. The repudiation of the specters is therefore central to the construction, performance, and maintenance of heteronormative gender subjectivity.

But what does it mean to think of queer bodies as ghosts?

Although Butler's work suggests that spectrality is a central mechanism in the production of normative gender, she does not explicitly spell out for us a feminist conception of spectrality. It is evident that Butler understands the abject to be ghosts that haunt the intelligible domain of gender as the limit of its possibility—a point that makes evident Butler's Foucauldian conception of the subject as an effect of operations and institutions of power. She thus primarily uses the notion of the specters of the abject to account for gender intelligibility as an effect of a violent exclusion, which is the contingent construction of gender. But this violent exclusion is productive because it is spectral—that is, the exclusion successfully regulates and maintains heteronormative gender because of its temporality. More specifically, the abject are the nonpresent presence that produces the domain of thinkable, livable, visible gendered subjects. When constructed and materialized in the temporal schema of spectrality, gender comes to distort and conceal not only its own production but also the reality of other possible or even actual configurations of gendered life. For this reason, gender comes to be understood in relationship to a heteronormative schema, which is generated through the spectrality of abject bodies.

Derrida (1994) suggests the present is always haunted by a nonpresent presence, a present absence. He offers up the notion of hauntology as a play on and deconstruction of ontology, suggesting that existence is never a pure presence but rather is a haunted state. Hauntology suggests that what is in the now is a product of ghosts that are invisible in the present. A specter, for Derrida, is a present absence constitutive of what is here and now; a specter is "a trace that marks the present with its absence in advance" (Derrida and Steigler 2002, 117). A specter thus produces and constrains the here and now through its very absence, which is itself an anticipatory temporality of potentiality: the specters could arrive. This temporal otherworldliness of specters—that they are beyond the present— is how they haunt and act on what is now. As social and cultural theorist Avery Gordon puts it, "Haunting describes how that which appears to be not there is often a seething presence, acting on and often meddling with the taken-for-granted realities." A specter, then, is "not a dead or missing person, but a social figure" that lurks in the periphery of the perceived and felt present (1997a, 8).

Reading Butler's account of the specters of the abject through Derrida suggests a hauntology of gendered existence. For both Butler and Derrida, the figure of the specter is a not-now that haunts the present. It is in the haunting that the present materializes. At the same time, that the specters are in the present means they render what is here and now unstable, threatening to expose the temporal current that underlies social life. The hauntology of gender reveals that heterogendered lives are ghost stories, lives that are produced through the disappearance of ghosts and the ever-present possibility of their appearance. What Derrida's account of the temporality of specters underscores about Butler's discussion of the specters of abjection is that heterogendered subjects appear as here only in repudiating what is not here.[5] It is the way nonnormativity temporally operates in the face of normativity that is central to the production and disciplining of gendered life. Hence, the threat of the specters of the abject is that they can disrupt the present and presence of heterogenders; they haunt the present presence of the gendered order with the threat of nonexistence. The haunting of social life or "the appearance of specters or ghosts is one way . . . we are notified that what's been concealed is very much alive and present" (Gordon 1997a, xvi). Because the potential arrival carries with it a threat to the present gendered order of things, those who occupy the domain of the abject are continuously excluded, erased, and pushed closer to nonexistence.

As queer feminist sociological scholarship shows, spectrality is regularly used and deployed in the contemporary concretization of lived gender (Pascoe 2007; Westbrook and Schilt 2015). In everyday social ritual, specters are called on to institute and regulate acceptable gender performance. C. J. Pascoe's influential qualitative account of the overuse of the epithet "fag" by boys against other boys—what she terms fag discourse—as a primary means to achieve American adolescent masculinity exemplifies the very real and material work of specters. "The fag discourse," Pascoe writes, "functioned as a constant reiteration of the fag's existence, affirming that the fag was out there; boys reminded themselves and each other that at any moment they could become fags if they were not sufficiently masculine" (2007, 60). According to Pascoe, explicit in the fag discourse is the specter of the fag, which functions as the discursive means by which the boys understood the possibility of their own impossibility. They engage in the ritual repudiation of the fag, as Butler's theory suggests they would, in order to performatively achieve the heterogendered subjectivity of masculine man.

Importantly, Pascoe's work shows that the specter is not merely an idea; the specter is rather a living ghost, an abject body that exists precariously in the realm of normative social life and that embodies the threat of non-existence. The consequences for such an embodiment are dire. The actual arrival of the specter of the (feminized) fag must be eliminated, and thus his existence is structured by actual violence because only in destroying the specter's arrival can the constitutive absence be maintained.[6] Even though the specter is always threatening, his arrival means exposure, and exposure means trouble for the gendered order. It is thus necessary for the specter to remain in the temporal mode of the present absence, which Pascoe's research shows is achieved through discursive and physical repudiation. Whereas those inside the heteronormative matrix of gender live the threat of nonexistence and violence through the specter, the living specter lives the reality of this violence. As that which can make trouble in the order of things, he must be destroyed.

The surplus of physical and existential violence in Pascoe's account of the specter of the fag is significant. It underscores that the temporality of the specter goes hand in hand with potential and actual violence. While gendered spectrality entails a normative threat of violence, violence is realized when the specter—the fag—actually shows up. In either case, as potential or actual, spectral violence operates as a central disciplinary mechanism of normative gender. It is the possibility (the threat) and confirmation (the living ghost) of nonexistence that keeps gendered subjects in a straight line.

That the queer specter is often the most apparent manifestation of gendered spectrality does not mean it is alone. As I have shown in the previous chapters, in the context of the United States, there are multiple ghost stories at the heart of normative gender. These ghost stories are inextricably linked to and enact the living histories of colonial processes of racialization and heterosexist domination, which are themselves bound to socioeconomic status and the demarcation of some bodies as healthy and normal and others as sick and abnormal. Andrea's experience with ghost stories underscores this relation between living histories and the dis-appearance of a multitude of ghosts. In fact, as Gayatri Spivak (1995) points out, certain specters must fail to appear as living ghosts in the Eurocentric global capitalist order in order for it to produce and maintain itself.[7] For Spivak, this failure gestures to the depth of nonexistence, namely that the materialization of social life depends on making some living ghosts far removed from presence—a removal that gestures to the depths of the present's violent undercurrent. Consequently, a consideration of the haunting of normative gender must take into account the multiplicity of ghost stories that operate to produce and constrain the field of gender that appears as livable. The specters of the abject are therefore just one kind of ghost that haunts gendered life.

In feminist scholarship, the threat of rape has not been considered as a gendered specter even though it has been shown to deeply constrain gendered life. To consider the threat of rape as spectral violence, to reframe how the threat operates in temporal terms, highlights how the very temporality of normative threats—their haunting—is a central way sexual domination is encrusted into the life of the feminine subject. This point is not meant to suggest that gendered specters do the exact same kind of gendered work, however. The threat of rape and the threat of the fag share a temporal structure and intent: to regulate and discipline gendered existence. But the way they concretely circulate and materialize, and what happens when they show up are distinct.

Spectral Violence and Feminine Existence

The centrality of the threat of rape to feminine existence produces deep existential fear (Griffin [1971] 1989; Brownmiller 1975; Gordon and Riger 1989; Ferraro 1996; Yavorsky and Sayer 2013). Susan Griffin's classic essay, "Rape: The All-American Crime," is one of the first to name the fear. She writes, "I have never been free of the fear of rape. From a very early age I, like most women, have thought of rape as part of my natural environment-something to be feared and prayed against like fire or lightning" ([1971] 1989, 422). Margaret Gordon and Stephanie Riger expand on this sentiment: "Most women experience fear of rape as a nagging, gnawing sense that something awful could happen, an angst that keeps them from doing things they want or need to do, or from doing them at the time or in the way they might otherwise do" (1989, 2). Contemporaneously, this idea of a female fear is often a sentiment shared by young women in my classrooms when talking about their experiences walking to their car or house at night while leaving a party, the library, or, really, almost any other public space. They have a cell phone in one hand and their keys ready in the other, in an attempt to be ready to fight and destroy the specter on their way to "safety," paradoxically the very place the specter is most likely to become real.

This gendered fear is not, however, paranoia. A coercive and violent institution of heterosexuality is an organizing principle of social life, personal experience, and gendered existence (Rich 1980; Bettcher 2006, 2007; Pascoe 2007). As an institution, this manifestation of heterosexuality produces specific ways of relating and feeling, of being affected, that become central to experience. In phenomenological terms, the institution of coercive and violent heterosexuality creates a general atmosphere shaping how things and people come to matter and what they feel like. That is, the institution of heterosexuality is generative of a mood that allows for one to make sense of the world, to understand how one is in the world, and to feel the world and the self in the world in a certain way.[8] The mood set by the institution of coercive and violent heterosexuality for girls and women in particular shrouds their lives in anxieties, concerns, and everyday experiences of sexualized vulnerability and danger (Phillips 2000; Pascoe 2007; Hlavka 2014). This institution thus generates the mood of fear in the lives of girls and women, leading them to cultivate practices of vigilance, to self-monitor, to be on high alert, and to deny their agency and desires. Paradoxically, this fear can also be a source of pleasure, but the fear is nevertheless constitutive. Understanding that there is a mood to the institution of coercive and violent heterosexuality draws attention to how certain ways of being affected become primary to the operation of the institution itself. That girls and women fear rape, even if an event of attempted or completed rape never occurs in one's life, is an effect of sensing the institution of coercive and violent heterosexuality.

While acknowledgment of the persistence of the fear of rape is important to uncovering an affective dimension of feminine existence, thinking of the fear of rape as a ghost helps underscore how rape haunts a woman's sense of self as free and turns her into a feminine existence. This hauntology of feminine existence reveals the temporal harm of rape culture and how that temporal harm is an integral part of the maintenance of feminine existence, perhaps most especially in a concrete situation when girls and women occupy the space of their bodies and the space around them in resistant and emancipatory ways.

From a feminist phenomenological view, the threat and fear of rape become lodged in the lived body such that they are formative to the appearance of a feminine body (Young 1980; Cahill 2001). In racialized feminine gestures like sitting compactly or moving without extension or ease in space, the lurking ghost of rape dis-appears as a generative character in the actualization of a feminine body as a previctim (Cahill 2001, 160). There is a deep paradox in the generation of the previctim, however. She may be constrained by fear and thus existentially violated, but the very embodiment of the previctim is that which renders her intelligible and desirable as a woman in a heterosexist society. Thus, the fear of rape generates a negated body that is also paradoxically a positive project of becoming a woman. She appears as an intelligible woman through the disappearance (both a psychological process of internalization and a cultural process of erasure and dismissal) of sexual domination, which entangles her in a contradictory web of powerlessness and empowerment produced by the same normative threat of rape.[9] That pleasure and sexual violation are woven together is why many girls and women "flirt with danger"—that is, are aroused by and desire their own sexual violability at the same time that they try to fight it (Phillips 2000, 100).[10]

However, the reason the threat is so successful, the reason it has and continues to enforce feminine existence, is not just because becoming the previctim is desirable in a heteromasculinist erotic and social order. Rather, the threat works so well in large part because it is violence that haunts existence. It is the present absence of rape, the possibility that it is yet to come, that makes the threat so potent. To be more concrete about this claim, imagine twenty-two-year-old Andrea's psychic life of ghost stories about rape. These stories and images swirling around in her body-mind are memories that set up or frame her existence. As a girl, the narrative practice of turning cautionary tales about rape into ghost stories was a coping mechanism, but it also was and remains a disciplinary mechanism. What Andrea learned as a girl and can recall as an adult is that her life has been haunted by rape. Even if she no longer tells such ghost stories, the haunting has temporally structured her existence. That she can recollect the prevalence of the specter of rape in her girlhood reveals its constitutive power. The residue of the haunting from girlhood is that Andrea knows and feels that something could happen to her.

While feminist legal scholar Catharine MacKinnon has argued that the "threat of sexual assault is threat of punishment for being female," my understanding and naming of the threat as spectral violence suggests that the threat is itself punishment (1989, 245). For MacKinnon, the prevalence of rape in society is not merely an affirmation of men's power over women; it also "defines what a woman *is*" (178). Although historically the prevalence of the threat and rape go hand in hand, the spectrality of the threat suggests that rape's absence also defines what a woman is in a sexist society. Of course, it is undeniable that girls and women are likely to be survivors of rape, making the prevalence of rape in their lives, as MacKinnon suggests, a mark of being a woman. Paradoxically, however, it is in the absence of rape that a feminine existence also appears. It is the prevalence of the specter of rape in a woman's life that defines, disciplines, and punishes her. In Andrea's life, what matters here is not that she is a survivor of rape, but that she could be raped and might be raped in the future. It is this anticipation of rape that marks her existence in a deeply meaningful way. What makes this mark a gendered one is not only that it is possible to situate Andrea's experience within a surplus of quantitative and qualitative data that underscore her anticipation as a shared experience among girls and women, but also, and this is the point that is most important to my analysis, that her anticipation (a kind of temporality in itself) is a continual deferral of her claim to freedom as a woman. The specter of rape disrupts the relation a woman has to an open future, and in doing so, to refer back to my analysis of the temporality of femininity in chapter 1, she becomes a feminine existence.

Thus, the ontological and physical burden of feminine existence is not that it is purely an oppressed or sexually objectified present presence. Rather, a feminine existence is a gendered existence whose future is under surveillance and disrupted by the specter of rape. It is the present absence of rape—the temporality of the normative threat—that constitutes the lived present of feminine existence. This constitutive present absence uncovers a disjointed temporality at the heart of feminine existence. The continual return of the specter inaugurates fear and apprehension because it discloses a vulnerability, a trace of absence, in the present. In a rape culture, the vulnerability is that in the future, one might be and is likely to be a survivor of rape. A woman feels this in the present through the specter's absence. Her potential nonexistence lies at the very core of how she is. To live with the ghost of rape, to be existentially haunted by it, is to have an impossibility traced through the actuality of one's present. This absence of rape at the heart of the present discloses the terror that lurks alongside women's future. This is precisely what Andrea discloses when she says, "I remember it was really scary . . . we knew something really awful could happen to little girls like us . . . we were all really scared" (Phillips 2000, 56).

Certainly there are important differences between the specters of the abject and the specter of rape. The specters of the abject are repudiated bodies whose possible presence terrorizes, and in turn inaugurates, violence against the abject. The normative threat of their appearance is not a threat of physical violation; it is an existential threat. The possibility of physical violence does, though, circumscribe the lives of the abject. In contrast, the specter of rape is an existential threat and a threat of physical violation. The ghosts who make up this specter are largely historical constructs of white supremacist heteropatriarchy. Though the construction of the specter of rape threatens the lives of people who appear to fit the construct (for example, men of color), in the lives of girls and women, the specter is a double threat: the possibility of physical and existential harm. The specter of rape is a residual promise of a woman's nonexistence at the heart of her existence. This a temporal promise; it is a promise that one's future might be impossible. To live this promise is to live as if the (black male) rapist is always already waiting to jump out of the bushes or attack you from behind as you walk down the street.

Among those who are situated as, are perceived to be, or are girls and women and whose lives are used to demarcate "acceptable" womanhood, the lived experience of the specter of rape is not homogeneous. As I have argued in previous chapters, historical constructs of white supremacy and heterosexism shape and constrain the way woman is lived, which means that rape haunts women in different ways according to their positioning in the hierarchical social order. For instance, to be a woman who inhabits multiple marginalized positions means that one endures a spectral violence produced by the convergence of multiple systems of power.[11] When a young white cis woman on a college campus fears rape as she walks from the library to her off-campus apartment late at night, she is being affected by the institution of violent and coercive heterosexuality, which makes her safe arrival at her apartment—her future—feel tenuous. If this cis woman is a woman of color, her fear of rape and thus her anxiety over her future is already entangled with fears about racist violence. When a trans woman on that same campus fears rape as she walks from the library to her off-campus apartment at night, because she lives under the same atmosphere of violent heterosexuality as the cis woman, she will also fear rape as a woman and her relation to her apartment, to her future, also feels fragile. At the same time, however, she might also be worried about being "found out" and therefore worried about whether or not she will experience transphobic violence—violence that relies on the same logic as the institution of violent heterosexuality but that is also distinct (Bettcher 2006, 2007). When gendered existence is lived under a regime of violent heterosexuality, whoever appears to be a woman, whoever is potentially visible as a woman—even if one does not (always) understand oneself as a woman—might experience the specter of rape, which then reifies the way feminine existence structures life, even at the very instance one refuses the category of woman or its normative construction. Thus, it is possible to make a connection between the distinct manifestations of the haunting and the enforcement of feminine existence in particular, and normative gender more generally. The specter of rape aims to restrict and regulate the field of possibility. It aims to limit one's future. Even in different manifestations of the specter of rape, the specter does not change its temporal logic or temporal intent: the specter of rape intends to trace nonexistence at the heart of existence. It raises the question and poses the threat of whether or not one will have a future of her own.

In *Being and Time* (1962), Martin Heidegger claims that the mood of anxiety, a generalized angst about the reality of one's death, gives meaning to a subject's existence through awareness of the possibility that she will cease to live. This awareness is, for Heidegger, an authentic relation to death insofar as it urges one to embrace the singularity of his existence and to posit a particular selfhood. In other words, in my anxiety, produced through the perception of a world without me, I come to make a world that is mine. In turn, I also embrace my own nonexistence and live authentically toward death. In contrast, an inauthentic relation to death and thus to one's subjectivity is lived through a fear of death. To fear one's own nonexistence, Heidegger argues, is to be trapped in the temporality of waiting; it is to wait for the arrival of the event and to never live a singular and free existence. Following Heidegger, it is possible to see how fear itself works to foreclose a future for girls and women; in doing so, it binds them to the passive present. Living the fear of rape is to live the fear of one's nonexistence, which is to be mired in the temporality of waiting—the very temporality of feminine existence. What makes the spectrality of the fear so important, however, is that in escaping presence, the fear remains. Unlike the fear of concrete objects, which can be removed to prevent and eliminate fear, the absence of the specter of rape sediments the fear in girls' and women's lives. As a consequence, the sediment of feminine existence remains.

Trauma Temporality

Understanding the temporal character of trauma reveals how disturbing the temporal effect of the specter of rape is. Although Gordon makes the distinction between haunting and trauma on the basis that haunting is a something to be done and trauma is a something that has been done (Gordon 1997a, xvi), I want to suggest that the temporality of the "to be done" in the case of haunting, although distinct from the temporality of the "has been" of trauma, is best understood as a degree of "has been" done. The temporal effects of spectrality and trauma make this connection clear. According to feminist psychiatrist and trauma expert Judith Herman, traumatic events are ones that "overwhelm the ordinary systems of care that give people a sense of control, connection, and meaning" (1992, 33). What makes trauma different from commonplace misfortunes, Herman explains, is that the former destroys or threatens the structures of the world that give life meaning and secure one's existential and physical integrity, while the latter pose problems or obstacles that are more readily ameliorated. In this context, trauma is not constituted by the mere presence of physical violation but is in large part an existential violation, one that may or may not coincide with distinct and visible physical assault. One of the deepest wounds and marks of trauma is that it undoes one's experience of time. As Herman explains it, traumatic events are interruptions in chronological time, namely interruptions of the past, which threaten the life or bodily integrity of a person. Trauma entails a "rupture in continuity between present and past," making the present markedly distinct from and dissociated from the past (89). Prolonged, repeated trauma is also an "obliteration of the future" (89). Traumatic events thus fundamentally alter the self not only physically but also through a temporal alteration that restructures and reorients the self. As I mention in the introduction, this alteration often means trauma subjects are "frozen in time" (Burstow 2003, 133). This is the temporal and existential effect of the specter of rape.

In chapter 1, drawing on Beauvoir, I argued that the temporality of feminine existence—the passive present—severs a woman from her past and forecloses her future, anchoring her to a cyclical present. This experience of the present, as Beauvoir puts it, freezes time. What spectral violence does is impose and enforce this temporality as a structure in girls' and women's lives, even as and perhaps precisely when they (could) act in defiance of normative gender and their own oppression. The spectral violence is a reminder of their potential nonexistence, but insofar as it overwhelms an open structure of time—the configuration of the structure of care itself, as Heidegger would have it[12]—the specter of rape also enacts trauma. In doing so, spectral violence freezes time. This ordinary terror is a mechanism that hurls a girl or woman into the passive present, actualizing the temporal structure of feminine existence. The specter intends to make a feminine existence out of a woman, thus underscoring a connection between the temporality of feminine existence and a key temporal effect of trauma. To become a feminine existence is to become a traumatized subject.

This is not to say, however, that the trauma of spectral violence is the same kind of trauma as that endured by survivors of rape. But it is possible to understand spectral violence as what clinical psychologist Maria Root (1992) calls insidious trauma. For Root, insidious trauma names the ongoing negative experiences and relentless forms of malice endured by members of an oppressed group, expanding the definition of and criteria for what counts as trauma. In a sexist or misogynist society, insidious trauma is accumulated over the course of women's lives and is no less destructive to the self than discrete traumatic events. Indeed, women routinely live the trauma of domestic captivity, "rendered captive by economic, social, psychological, and legal subordination, as well as by physical force" (Herman 1992, 76).[13]

That the specter manifests trauma's temporal effect is nothing short of significant. Indeed, this relationship between spectral violence and trauma suggests a shared continuum of trauma between those who endure the threat and those who endure rape. Feminist philosopher Susan Brison recounts her own trauma as a survivor of a brutal rape, underscoring in particular the temporal shattering endured in rape's aftermath. "For the first several months after my attack," Brison writes, "I led a spectral existence, not quite sure whether I had died and the world went on without me, or whether I was alive but in a totally alien world" (2002, 9). This spectral mode of being, a limbo between life and death, is what Brison goes on to call a shattered life, a loss of security, control, and trust. This loss constitutes a new present for the survivor of trauma. The survivor of rape finds herself shattered from her past wherein the world felt safe, and instead she is now anchored in the present without "assurance that she will be able to avoid [rape] in the future" (10). Thus, the survivor's relation to time, and in particular her relation to an open future, is haunted by rape—by the rape she endured, by reliving its memory in her body, by the possibility of enduring it again. The rape she endured becomes a form of spectral violence itself.

Although she does not frame it for us in this way, Brison's spectral existence echoes the passive present of feminine existence. The temporal hiatus diminishes her claim to her self as free (what Brison might refer to as in control and secure) and binds her to a present without connection to her past and future. The major difference, however, between the survivor of rape and the ordinary experience of spectral violence is that surviving rape hurls Brison into an existence whose nonexistence cuts even deeper because it brings the specter closer to her existence. He is a presence. Rather than a residual threat, rather than being an absence, the survivor of rape has endured and continues to endure her nonexistence through the presence of the rapist. Because the trauma of rape shatters the self by making nonexistence a presence, the survivor's healing in the present relies on regaining control of her future. A new relation to the future is the only way to successfully banish the presence of the specter.

According to Brison, regaining this relation to the future is especially hard for the survivor of rape. The frequent victim blaming of a rape culture leaves survivors facing "an especially intractable double-bind: they need to know there's something they can do to avoid being similarly traumatized in the future, but if there *is* such a thing, then they blame themselves for not knowing it (or doing it) at the time" (2002, 74).[14] Whereas Brison emphasizes the burden of responsibility or overwhelming helplessness this bind places on survivors of rape, it is also the case that there is another significant bind girls and women who are survivors of rape find themselves in: to be a girl or a woman in a sexist or misogynist society is to live with the specter of rape. For the survivor of rape who is trying to regain a future, she is practically set up to fail. If the specter of rape is a disciplinary mechanism that imposes and enforces the temporality of feminine existence, then a girl or woman who survives rape faces at least a double haunting—that of the trauma of rape and that of the specter. A survivor's possibility to regain a relation to the future is always already jeopardized. In contemporary society, that future is further jeopardized by the prevalence of the filming, circulation, and replaying of rapes on social media (Heyes 2016). Moreover, if a survivor's rape is one that fits the white supremacist mythical narrative of rape, rebuilding an emancipatory future is uncertain insofar as that narrative itself preempts emancipatory lived gender.[15]

As distinct from the trauma of rape itself, the specter of rape is an ordinary haunting that makes its victims feel out of control, insecure, and anxious about what the future holds. The specter begs its victims to experience the world as unsafe, to live a heightened vulnerability, to worry, to be apprehensive, and ultimately to live in fear. Such a condition, etched in the living body, is arguably a primary way in the contemporary United States that feminine existence remains a presence in girls' and women's lives. The road to healing the subjective wound of the specter of rape is undoubtedly different from healing other forms of trauma. But that it encrusts the temporality of feminine existence into the heart of lived gender means that negotiating the effect of the specter also requires regaining a relation to the future.

Of course, neither survivors of rape nor girls and women who live only the threat of the specter are mere victims. Brison's testimony is just one example of resilience, healing, and possibility in the face of trauma. It is possible to work to regain a relation to the future. Yet the imposition of the temporality of feminine existence, which can be understood as a trauma temporality itself, means this relation to the future is much more difficult to ascertain.

So how does one gain a relation to the future that was not hers for the taking to begin with?

Feminist Futures: A Life without Ghosts

Ghostbusting.

In September 2014, Columbia University undergraduate student Emma Sulkowicz began a feminist performance art project entitled *Mattress Performance (Carry That Weight)* for her senior thesis in visual arts. The project was a protest against rape on campus and her own survival of campus rape that went unrecognized by Columbia. For nine months, Sulkowicz carried around a fifty-pound dorm room mattress, a symbol of the place in and on which she was raped, often with the physical support of other young women. At a time when rape, and campus rape in particular, surfaced on the national stage with the Obama administration and Vice President Joe Biden forming the It's On Us campaign, Sulkowicz's performance engendered a firestorm of controversy, criticism, and praise. She was celebrated for engaging in political protest, publicizing trauma, challenging institutional neglect, and refusing to remain silent in the face of injustice and rape culture. She was criticized for shaming a fellow student without proof, for engaging in disruption and disrespect, and for misusing and debasing art for malicious purposes. From this feminist's view, it is evident that Sulkowicz's performance shocked and disturbed the ordinary perceptual faith in college campuses as safe havens for the cultivation of young women's agency. She exposed the weight of rape, the weight of living with the trauma of rape, of being haunted by rape, of carrying its weight around in the present. The exposure of rape's absence in the present—that is, in making it a presence, which Sulkowicz does with the mattress—challenges the temporal logic of spectral violence. *Mattress Performance* is an event of the untimely, a surfacing of ghosts that structure existence but are ordinarily hidden in the present presence of things. As such, Sulkowicz's performance is an act of feminist ghostbusting.

Insofar as the efficacy of spectral violence lies in its capacity to evade perception in the present (that is, it remains an absence), the event of the untimely is an integral act of resistance to a rape culture and to feminine existence. An event of the untimely is that which draws forth the absences, the ghosts, the invisible and forgotten aspects of existence to inaugurate change. Ghostbusting refers to uncovering the affective, material, and historical conditions that constrain, police, and enforce normative gender. This has long been a central feminist task. But more specifically in terms of temporality, ghostbusting refers to a rupture in the present presence of things—the way things are—that necessitates a temporal shift. The visible presence of the mattress, for instance, conjures up, in a material way, the living ghosts that haunt Sulkowicz. Since it is their absence that is productive, in conjuring ghosts, in making them a presence, it is possible to undo their structural and temporal weight in the present. While a feminist practice of conjuring ghosts might sound like a magical or mystical politics that cannot touch material reality, the very point of this chapter has been to show how ghosts are not mere apparitions but rather have significant material effects and are themselves a kind of materiality. A feminist politics focused on conjuring ghosts is not a disembodied or insubstantial politics but instead is one that exposes what has been covered over, hidden, and excluded from appearing. However, the exposure is not merely to show the exclusion; the exposure aims to restructure time itself. Thus, ghostbusting is not just the uncovering of previously hidden, unrecognized, or invalidated knowledge and experiences. It is also the disruption of the hidden structures of temporality that actualize the field of normative gender.

In contrast to the untimeliness of gendered specters that maintain the order of things, feminist philosopher Elizabeth Grosz (2004) suggests a transformative event of the untimely is a disruption to what is perceived in the now. As I will discuss further in the next chapter, Grosz insists that the untimely is transformative when the deep past activates to challenge the present. Such a challenge generates an opening up of that which has previously been closed off, concealed, constrained, and conditioned. Importantly, the past need not be understood as only the historical past. The past is also the anonymous, the absences, the invisible depths of existence. In the broadest sense, ghostbusting refers to one mode of feminist temporal resistance that aims to disrupt the operation of temporality that harms and confines. Because the temporal harm is simultaneously past and present, challenging the ways the past elides the present and the ways the present draws on the past is central to the practice of ghostbusting. As is the case with *Mattress Performance*, exposing what underlies the present, what is endured in the present as an absence, is one way to summon the ghosts. In doing so, it makes it possible to bust them out of time.

Neither Butler nor Derrida conceives of specters as mere constraint. For Derrida, the arrival of the specter is the possibility for justice. For Butler, the presence of the abject is the condition of possibility for subversion. In making the absence of spectral violence a presence, as Sulkowicz does, there is an exposure of and thus an opening in the temporal constraint of gendered existence that holds promise. Turning the absence into a presence, bringing the specters out of the shadows, offers the potential to destroy their productive status so that new gendered possibilities can be realized. This temporal shift is the promise of a new time, an existence in which girls like Andrea may no longer have to tell ghost stories.

If, as I have argued throughout this book, the living histories of racialized, heterosexist sexual domination structure and are encrusted in the living body, then what is needed to sustain the promise of the untimely is a sustained feminist political practice of ghostbusting. That is, what is needed is a way to enact and embody a feminist politics of temporality. A feminist temporality must be one that refigures the content of that which is not-presence in order to realize an open relation to the past, present, and future. Yet existence is never a pure presence. There are always absences, anonymous undercurrents, and temporal gaps that are central to life, and to the ability to embody a relation to the future. What is needed, then, is an affective temporal resistance that touches embodied experience in the tacit ways that structures of domination do.

Part III

The Future

Reclaiming my time. What he failed to tell you was, when you're on my time I can reclaim it.

—Maxine Waters, July 27, 2017

6

Feminist Politics and the Difference of Time

Feminist struggles of all kinds aim to produce a breach between the overwhelming weight of the patriarchal (or racist) past, its disruption in the present . . . and its overcoming in the future.

—Elizabeth Grosz, *The Nick of Time*

Those who have an interest in perpetuating the present always shed tears for the marvelous past about to disappear.

—Simone de Beauvoir, *The Second Sex*

On January 1, 2018, a group of Hollywood celebrities founded the Time's Up movement to draw attention to the pervasive reality and history of sexual assault and harassment of working women.[1] But it was Oprah Winfrey's acceptance speech for the Cecil B. DeMille award at the Golden Globes just one week later that made the politics of time central to the celebrity movement visible: "For too long, women have not been heard or believed if they dared to speak their truth to the power of those men. But their time is up. Their time is up. Their time is up. . . . So I want all the girls watching here and now to know that a new day is on the horizon!" (Russonello 2018). Neither this movement nor its politics of time is necessarily new, however. It was only three months earlier that the Me Too movement became a viral means of resistance to the way sexual domination is a structural feature of women's existence.[2] The contemporary student-led activist movement against campus rape preceded the Time's Up and Me Too movements by several years.[3] In 2006 Tarana Burke launched the original Me Too campaign. And, almost forty years earlier, Catharine MacKinnon (1979) published her groundbreaking text on the widespread practice and systematic erasure of the sexual harassment of working women and Take Back the Night marches became a central practice of feminist resistance to sexual violence against women. Thus, these recent movements are part of a legacy of feminist resistance efforts to the various forms of sexual domination that are central to women's lives and that, as I have argued in this book, structure and maintain a violent schema of gender. Like past efforts, Time's Up and Me Too are events that aim to interrupt the normal operation of things as well as the normative order and structure of existence, namely the reality and concealment of sexual domination in girls' and women's lives. Insofar as these feminist movements attempt to uncover what is covered up in the past and present, they are, like resistance efforts before them, untimely events. They generate disorder in the order of time that produces and maintains the reality of sexual domination.

Like the ones prior, these recent movements raise familiar questions. Is this a watershed moment? Is this a time that will make a difference?

Since the event is still at work, these are questions that cannot yet be answered. But the event still prompts reflection. What is at stake in this moment of resistance is the making possible of a different sense of temporality. Although time is always at stake in feminist politics—indeed, feminism is all about changing time—that time is an explicit theme in the Time's Up movement makes it particularly interesting. In this chapter, I argue that what matters for a feminist politics is not merely that sexual domination ends but also that a necessary condition for that end to come is the reconfiguration of temporality. If the time of domination is indeed to be up, the lived experiences of time must change. Thus, the question I am interested in is this: How will this time make a difference in how we live time?

A central theme of this book is the way temporality is a gendered structure and experience of sexual domination. More specifically, I show how particular relations to time and habits of temporality institute and sediment racialized sexual domination in the lived experience of feminine existence, which in turn constrains the field of lived gender by reifying normative gender. To live gender in ways that sediment racialized heteropatriarchy into the collective milieu does not require overt acts of domination. Rather, it is a temporal undercurrent of experience that tacitly conspires to keep power alive in us. This conspiracy between temporality, gender, race, and sexual domination demands a feminist politics of temporality, a resistance that harnesses and reconfigures how time is lived, how time is embodied, and how it affects existence. Such a politics is necessary to busting out of the closed temporal schemas of a sexually violent, racialized, heterogendered system.

In order to understand the gravity of a feminist politics of temporality, I first offer a phenomenological consideration of temporality as affect by drawing on Lisa Guenther's critical phenomenology of solitary confinement and discussions of temporality in trauma theory. Building on the temporal politics of ghostbusting I advanced in chapter 5, I then consider three experiences of time that are necessary for interrupting the collective and subjective actualization of feminine existence. I first argue for the need for untimely events that interrupt the ordinary operation of temporality. I turn to feminist appropriations of Henri Bergson, namely to Elizabeth Grosz's (2004, 2005) discussion of the virtual leap and Alia Al-Saji's (2014) phenomenology of hesitation, to show how untimely events affectively thwart the movement of the sedimented past into the present. In other words, untimely events disrupt habit. Second, although the past must be interrupted, a particular phenomenological recovery of the past is required to undo the temporality of feminine existence. I draw on Guenther's (2013) discussion of the experience of doing time when living death in solitary confinement in order to argue that feminist strategies for creating conditions of temporal subjectivity through recovery of the past are necessary for the concretization of freedom. Last, drawing on queer theory, I conclude with a consideration of the significance of a habit of indeterminacy to a feminist politics of temporality.

In no way is this an exhaustive account of temporal modes of resistance. My aim is to show the difference temporality makes and why it must be central to feminist politics. However, I account for these three particular experiences of time because I take them to fracture and keep open the temporal structures of gendered existence, thus holding the promise of living a new dawn.[4]

Temporality and Affection

In *Solitary Confinement*, Lisa Guenther's (2013) analysis of the existential harm of incarceration concretizes the phenomenological claim that temporality is a central structure of experience. Guenther refers to temporality as a hinge of subjectivity that is acutely undermined by solitary confinement. Indeed, what makes solitary confinement so deeply troubling, Guenther suggests, is that it thwarts the temporal structure of subjectivity by immobilizing time. Prisoners in solitary are likely "to get stuck in a moment that goes nowhere, closed into a circular repetition of the same" (215). In effect, "the solitary subject literally comes unhinged" not only because the subject is forced into a physical withdrawal from the world but also because solitary freezes a subject's relation to time (213). The unhinging that solitary confinement realizes so well is, Guenther shows, predicated on destroying the hinge of temporality. While prolonged isolation itself threatens the intersubjective condition of human existence, the affective power of solitary confinement is its destruction of the temporal structure of subjectivity. As Guenther puts it, "To be a temporal subject is to maintain a creative relation to one's own temporal Being-in-the-world" such that to be unhinged—that is, to be refused a temporal subjectivity—is to paradoxically live death (219). The efficacy of solitary is not about merely being alone; it is about being isolated in time.

From a phenomenological perspective, experience and existence are temporally structured. Following Husserl (1991), the classical phenomenological claim is that this structuring is triadic; there is a perceptual field of what appears (the present) that actualizes through horizons of retention (the past) and protention (the future). What critical phenomenological claims, like Guenther's and Beauvoir's, suggest is that this triadic structure is not pregiven and immutable; rather, its distortion and manipulation temporally restructure and reframe experience. This warping of the triadic temporal structure undermines subjectivity and conditions how a person feels and assumes the world as a field of possibility. To isolate a subject in a redundant present, which happens, albeit quite differently, for the prisoner in prolonged solitary confinement and to those hurled into a feminine existence, is to destroy the temporal hinge between a subject and the world. It is, to use Guenther's language, to live death.

For Guenther, time becomes unhinged in experiences of severe bodily deprivation. This unhinging compounds and sediments the harm of solitary such that the harm is the deprivation of contact with others as well as the resulting destruction of a subject's time. The prolonged deprivation of isolation produces a temporal delay that makes the prisoner fall out of synch with her own subjectivity. However, it is important to acknowledge that depriving a subject of an open relation to time is itself a form of bodily deprivation that is deeply affective as domination. The manipulation and loss of time endured by a prisoner becomes its own kind of deprivation. The combination of bodily deprivation–temporal unhinging is the harm and torture of solitary confinement. In such a life, if it is a life at all, temporality becomes not only a structure that conditions experience but also a way to affectively alter the way a person feels.

That the breakdown of temporality can itself be a bodily deprivation is not lost on Guenther. As she shows in her discussion of resistance to living death, it is in coping with and managing time that prisoners find ways to survive the violence of confinement. To understand that time plays a central role in survival underscores that temporality is not just a structure of subjectivity but is also a mode of affection. That is, a certain relation to and experience of time is something one must feel in order to posit oneself as a subject.

Trauma theory (Herman 1992; van der Kolk 2015) helps elucidate a conception of temporality as affection. While physiologically and psychologically trauma is endured in the living body in various ways, a central feature and consequence of trauma is the way it distorts and damages one's relation to time. While an experience of a rape might leave neurobiological imprints such that a victim may lack emotional response, have a fragmented memory, may experience emotional instability, and so forth, she will also be deeply affected by the reorganization of her relation to time. As Judith Herman remarks, "Traumatized people feel and act as though their nervous systems have been disconnected from the present" (1992, 35). This feeling of disconnect from the present is an effect of trauma as an overwhelming past (Herman 1992; Brison 2003). Insofar as this disconnect is felt, indeed it registers in the nervous system, and inasmuch as it binds one to her trauma, this temporal affection becomes a form of trauma in itself. The distortion of the triadic structure through trauma's rupture is lived and felt as trauma, not merely its effect. This point is not meant to suggest that trauma's harm is only temporal. Rather, it underscores the parasitic relationship between trauma and temporality because it highlights temporality as affect and how it can function as a weapon and means of trauma or domination.

Accordingly, and this is a central claim in this book, one need not undergo physical or psychological trauma or torture to be harmed or disaffected by temporality. One can live gender through historical constructs and experiences of racialized heterosexist domination in such a way that one (prereflectively) lives and feels time as an unhinging of subjectivity. Although distinct from the experiences of prisoners and trauma victims, this lived experience of time is also a bodily deprivation that produces a particular feeling and mode of being affected. The affect of the temporality of feminine existence, for instance, traps one in a closed temporal structure, producing an autoaffect wherein one feels temporally thwarted. The temporal entrapment does not register consciously for the feminine subject but is sensed through what she can and cannot do and what can be done to her. One becomes temporally moved in a distinct way.

Her self-experience is always tied to a specific mode of heteroaffection wherein, in the temporal entrapment, one is always subjected to the possibility to be touched by others, regardless of her consent. This heteroaffection of the temporality of feminine existence perverts the intersubjective human condition—that we are always vulnerable to the touch of others—because it amplifies the vulnerability and undermines its shared dimension. The structure of the temporality of feminine existence is what makes this mode of heteroaffection possible and acceptable. It is a way of being moved, of feeling oneself moved. This temporality is a mode of affection by which one experiences her self through the way she can be touched by others. It conditions the possibility of such affect, but it is itself also affect insofar as the feminine subject need not actually be touched by others to touch and be touched by others in this way. When this affectivity intersects with racializing affect, one's touchability intensifies.

That gendered subjectivity is affected by its temporal structure points to the importance of a feminist politics of temporality. Temporality matters in how we live with others. To engage what temporality does to us and to fissure the way it sediments and actualizes systems of domination is to live time in resistance to racialized heteropatriarchy. Such a political effort means that feminist politics must always be a phenomenological politics directed at the pursuit of new ways to live time. In order to live time in feminist resistance and thus to pursue a liberatory temporal subjectivity, there are at least three dimensions of temporality that feminist efforts must challenge and reconfigure: the habit of normative gender, the harm of the temporality of feminine existence, and the deep sedimentation of normative gender.

Untimely Events

A strategic temporal resistance to heteronormative gender is at the heart of a Butlerian politics of queer performativity. For Butler, troubling the present and presence of gender requires "the parodic proliferation and subversive play of gendered meanings" ([1990] 1999, 46). This subversion undermines the stability and repetition of heteronormative gender through the continual disruption of the present. For Butler, subversive play exposes the fictional character of gender and actualizes new gendered possibilities, undermining the repetition and naturalization of heteronormativity. Thus, one central aspect of the political operation of queer performativity is to fissure and destabilize the temporal process of sedimentation. However, in the phenomenological account of sedimentation and gender that I offer in chapter 4, the habit of heteronormative gender is difficult to disrupt. If normative habit relies on immobility and is rigid because of its thick and forgotten past, such habit preempts the possibility for play and subversion. The very function of normative habit is to preclude queer performativity. Certainly, as Butler notes, the repetition of heteronormative gender is not always successful such that it is in the promise of failure that queer performativity has a chance. My concern, however, is what to do with the successful repetition—that is, the actualization of the habit—of normative gender. How does one disrupt a habit that is intensely recalcitrant and overdetermined, a habit that is directed by an inability to be disrupted?

Elizabeth Grosz's (2004, 2005) and Alia Al-Saji's (2014) appropriations of French philosopher Henri Bergson's discussion of temporality can help address this question. Although Grosz and Al-Saji take up Bergson in different ways, Grosz with the Bergsonian notion of the virtual past and Al-Saji with his address of hesitation, they do so because he offers a way to think the relation between temporality and affective transformation, or a becoming otherwise. On my reading, their turns to Bergson underscore a temporal feminist politics of delay or the need for untimely events. By turning to their considerations of untimely events, I underscore that delay (and efforts that enact delay) is a necessary temporal practice for the destruction of the obstinacy of normative habit.

The temporal concepts of the actual, virtual, and duration are central to Bergson's thinking. A discussion of the virtual first appears in his early text, *Time and Free Will* ([1889] 2001), and is developed to a much greater extent in *Matter and Memory* ([1896] 1990), where he addresses the virtual as the continuous and differentiating or heterogeneous quality of subjective existence. For Bergson, duration refers to a singular and plural movement, to the way a certain past stays or endures and to a simultaneity of plural past and present movements. Although duration does not determine the future, what is actual is assembled through a particular line or intensity of the past. This particular movement of the past stems from a temporal reservoir of the virtual. The virtual thus refers to a whole past or a plurality of pasts, indicating the different rhythms of existence that can actualize or become present. The endurance of a duration always exists alongside other durations, which means that the field of the actual is always multiple.

In *Matter and Memory*, Bergson pursues this connection between the actual, the virtual, and duration by accounting for their relation to memory and perception. He suggests that memory is recruited by the present in order to actualize the persistent becoming of the living body. It "is from the present that comes the appeal to which memory responds" such that my body acts, perceives, and actualizes a world ([1896] 1990, 153). Bergson distinguishes memory from bodily habit, arguing that the latter is a repetition that produces a body schema while memory is defined by the difference of singular pasts that fissure the actualization of habit. In contrast to bodily habit, which persists as an always ready to actualize interval between perception and action, memory is singular, specific, and undirected. Memory is latent potential. It is a movement toward the present from the indefinite virtual reservoir of the past. The creative power of memory is, for Bergson, that it draws on the whole past where different rhythms await actualization. As the subjective mode of access to the past, memory is the way the past comes to my present perception and extends into present action. This movement toward the present is the potential of radical divergence. Or, as Grosz puts it, with memory, the "present is fractured or nicked . . . by the past" (2004, 170).

For Bergson, the movement of memory to the present first requires a leap into the virtual, and it is this virtual leap that Grosz fashions as a political resource. On Bergson's account, the virtual leap is taken when normal perception fails. It is taken in those moments when there is tension between perception and expectation, when a problem presents itself, or when I sense that the present is not what I felt it was. When perceptual faith fails, for instance, I am hurled outside of normal perception, and to resolve the failure, I must make a leap into the past. The virtual leap is required when there is a "delay or rift between perception and future action" (Grosz 2005, 101). The leap is thus "a detachment of our attention from the present" and "is the preparatory gesture that readies us for specific recollections" (Grosz 2004, 179). If habit preempts access to the whole past, then the leap into the multiplicity of the past is an untimely action of resistance and creation insofar as the reservoir of memory can disrupt this present. The political potential of the virtual leap is that it is access to the past that "has not been directly utilized, used up, by the present" (186). Because the leap "carries no pregiven plan or guarantee except a derangement of the present order, a movement of rendering its order insecure and replaceable," the virtual leap holds the promise of nicking the present and, in turn, changing the future (186). In other words, the untimeliness of the leap is that it disorients a sedimented perceptual field.

Ultimately, according to Grosz, the virtual leap is a vital feminist effort because it opens up what is and could be. Access to the multiplicity of the past will fissure the presence of power because that presence relies on an occlusion of the virtual. Systems of power and domination elide the deep reservoir of the past in order to maintain their hold in the present, to keep intact what has been and still is. Accordingly, the virtual leap is necessary for reconfiguring present and future actualities. As Grosz puts it, the leap

> produces the resources for multiple futures, for open pathways, for indeterminable consequences, as well as for those regularities and norms that currently prevail. The present, with its structures of domination, has actualized elements, fragments of the past, while rendering the rest dormant, inactive, virtual. This means that the future, possible futures, have inexhaustible resources of the past, of that realm of the past still untouched by the present, to bring about a critical response to the present and ideally replace it with what is better in the future. (2004, 253)

Grosz's reading of Bergson's virtual leap as a political resource also draws attention to the political potential of delay. If bodily habit is generative of perception and action in the absence of delay, then the leap is inspired by a delay in habit. The delay of habit interrupts a particular integration and repetition of the past in the present, and in turn requires and opens up the past. The delay thwarts repetition and is suggestive of potential and creativity. Moreover, inasmuch as the leap requires a turn away from the habitual present, the leap itself is delay. Delay, then, not only suspends immediate action but also displaces immediate or habitual sensation with a feeling that something could be otherwise.

Although the habit of feminine existence is a thick past "imperiously breathed into" a living body "from the first years of her life" that is structured by an inability to change and that occludes other gendered modes of existence, it does not determine the virtual, and as a consequence is capable of change (Beauvoir 2010, 266).[5] The leap into the virtual is the way to open up the potential of gendered existence. Yet the habit of normative gender itself, because it is rigidly structured and directed, requires a critical interruption that enacts delay in order to affect the virtual leap. For Al-Saji, following Bergson, it is "the bodily experience of temporal hesitation" (2014, 143) that prevents the movement of habit and produces a transition from repetition to tendency, a potential to become otherwise. If Grosz's turn to the virtual leap offers a way to recruit another past, then Al-Saji's account of hesitation offers a way to critically interrupt obstinate habit that precludes such recruitment.

Al-Saji's phenomenology of hesitation considers the necessary temporal condition for interrupting rigid and recalcitrant affects that repeat historical racist schemas of perception and thus predetermine the future as the past. In other words, Al-Saji turns to hesitation to understand how to stop habits of domination that are directed at overdetermination rather than indetermination. On her reading of Bergson, "Hesitation defines the structure of time . . . the ontological interval wherein time makes a difference, wherein it acts in experience" (2014, 142). Hesitation is the temporality that slows down habit, thus producing a bodily affect that makes habit felt as habit. As Al-Saji puts it, "Hesitation is a deceleration that opens up the affective infrastructure of perception, in order both to make it responsive to what it has been unable to see and to make aware its contextual and constructed features" (147). Accordingly, the temporality of hesitation is an interrupting affect that cuts into habitual movement. This fracturing of habit does not cease and eliminate habit entirely; instead it substitutes habit with alternative modes of feeling, perceiving, and existing.

Hesitation is an affective delay that punctures habit. What makes hesitation possible in relation to the deep rigidity and immobility of normative habits is that hesitation itself is related to the indeterminacy of habit. While habits tend toward determination, they are laden with indeterminacy such that they are always susceptible to interruption. This structuring indeterminacy is where hesitation and habit coexist, even though habit's goal is to render that indeterminacy invisible and to override hesitating affect. Moreover, although normative habits of gender and race often generate a hesitant mode of existence, an experience of oneself as incapable of movement or as severed from agency, Al-Saji's point is that habits are always already entangled with a positive hesitancy, a hesitancy that is the potential for disruption. Since it is only with delay that normative habit is suspended and the field of perception and affection expands, what hesitation as a politics of temporal delay suggests is the urgency for continual interruption.

The delay, realized through hesitation, is therefore what conditions the virtual leap. In the absence of hesitation, the leap is improbable. But together these temporal moments offer the potential to reconfigure the past–present–future relation. It is this reconfiguration that makes them untimely. Their potential to disrupt the temporal structures of domination, which is to disorder the normative order of things, makes them a temporal inconvenience and unwelcome temporal efforts. Consequently, a feminist politics must be in the business of being ill timed in order to hold the temporal order at bay. In doing so, the field is set for the reorientation of the temporality of normative gendered habit.

From Time Warp to Doing Time

Freedom is always bound to an experience of time. Indeed, it is the temporal structure of feminine existence that in part preempts concrete freedom. As I detail in chapter 1, a central and implicit claim Beauvoir makes in *The Second Sex* is that the denial of freedom for those who assume a feminine existence is structured by and experienced through a loss of the past. Ruptures with the past, instituted by the imposition of heteroeroticism, hurl one into the temporality of the passive present, a distortion of human temporality that is lived as a theft of the future. These ruptures warp time in such a way that the feminine subject also loses a relation to freedom. This theft is bound to a racialized use and manipulation of time that crosses and produces the bodies of racialized subjects in ways that also destroy their temporal relation to freedom. Recovering and preventing the break with the past is thus central to realizing an embodied relation to the future for various modes of racialized, gendered existence. Accordingly, whereas I have just discussed the importance of the past as a transformative resource, here I underscore the urgency of healing the loss of the past in order to gain a future. Recovering and building this temporal relation to the past and future requires efforts to do time.

Guenther's discussion of prisoners' resistance to the temporal experience of living death elucidates the existential and political significance of efforts to live time when time has been stolen or broken. From a prisoner's situation, survival relies on doing time "rather than allowing the time to 'do you'" (2013, 214). Doing time when one is sentenced to and thus confined by time, Guenther argues, is not only a way to distract one from an impoverished relation to time but is also a way to reconstitute a temporal subjectivity. Doing time allows prisoners to cope with the psychological and existential deterioration of the self that results from their temporal and physical incarceration. The strategies of doing time when incarcerated include time management, which allows one to control one's own time in the face of being controlled, and world-making activities, like creating art or studying, that impart a sense of meaning and futurity to one's confined existence. Regardless of the specificity of the strategy, it is vital to do time in the face of it doing you because "using time, feeling in control of time . . . is a matter of affirming oneself as a temporal subject rather than just an object persisting over time" (219).

Interestingly, Beauvoir describes coping mechanisms and protests that are undertaken to survive the isolation of the temporality of feminine existence. The married woman, for instance, "locked into the conjugal community . . . has to," Beauvoir claims, "change this prison into a kingdom" (2010, 470). To resist her imprisonment, "she encloses faraway countries and past times within her four walls in the form of more or less earthly flora and fauna," and she will invest time in decorating and maintaining the home "as an expression of her personality" because "it is she who has chosen, made, and 'hunted down' furniture and knickknacks" (471). Ultimately these material practices attempt to turn one's confinement to immanence, manifested concretely in the relegation to the home, into a world-making effort. They are efforts to resist being done in. These efforts are not utterly futile. A woman might gain small victories in the confines of the house that can generate what Bonnie Mann (2008) refers to as "a woman's point of view," a critical way of perceiving the world that fissures subordination and opens up the possibility of resistance and redemption. In the end, however, Beauvoir is dismissive of such efforts; indeed, she explicitly refers to them as doing nothing. For Beauvoir, the wife's effort to turn the prison into a kingdom further mires her in the temporality of feminine existence because the efforts cannot signify or constitute a world for the woman. They cannot reach out toward the future because they tend toward maintaining, not destroying, the prison. The temporal character of the efforts ultimately makes them ineffective.[6] They are not ways of doing time but instead reconstitute the very operation of time as confinement. The feminine subject cannot escape her temporal confinement through practices that reify her situation.

What matters, then, is the way resistance efforts tend to living time. What Guenther's (2013) account of doing time highlights is that temporal resistance must tend toward healing what has been ruptured. For instance, while the incarcerated subject is not liberated by doing time—indeed, the prisoner can only sustain himself—the efforts to regain a social relation to time and a temporal existence do make a difference in the prisoner's existence. That one can do time, rather than be done in by it, is a matter of surviving a living death. Even though there are moments when these two can become one and the same, one should not equate a gendered sentence to a life sentence in solitary confinement.[7] Yet Guenther's account of how prisoners in solitary do time in order to not be done in by it highlights the necessity of recuperating a ruptured temporality. The material constraints on prisoners makes their doing only "partial solutions or coping mechanisms" (2013, 220). In spite of the incompleteness, however, their efforts gesture toward the importance of doing time to resist subjection and underscore how to do time in ways that make a difference.

If one can grant that the feminine subject is also being done in by time, then she must find ways to do time to become a temporal subject. She needs to realize efforts that allow her to temporalize and she needs conditions in which she can undertake such efforts. In order for a woman to constitute herself as a freedom, to temporalize freedom, the particular way her time has been warped must be challenged. She must find ways to recover and live her past in order to do time in ways that challenge the confinement instituted by her gendered existence. For the feminine subject, to do time is to push back on the imposition of the temporal confinement; it is to undermine the material efforts to steal her time. Although I certainly do not mean to suggest that doing time in resistance to the imposition of feminine existence is sufficient for the realization of freedom, doing time in the face of domination will fissure its very structure and thus opens up the possibility for a relation to the future. In contrast to those who are incarcerated, doing time in the face of the imposition of feminine existence is a way not just to cope with domination; rather, it is a way to displace the ticking of its clock. Since the subject is time, how she does her time makes all the difference. Importantly, because of the way feminine existence is produced through and against other temporalities of domination, this feminist doing of time will challenge the entire temporal operation of power.

Doing time is not an effort that begins one day and ends another. Efforts to generate and recuperate a temporal subjectivity by tending to the lived past are about critical resistance and world-making in the face of domination—although to heal one's broken temporality does not mean that one could never be done in again. Temporal subjectivity requires a continual effort to make use of time in ways that open up the relation between the past, present, and future. A feminist practice thus creates and sustains the temporality of freedom. This means that a new lived relation to the past must not be one that merely anchors a subject to the past. The lived past must resist the temptation of inflexible habit, which makes existence unreflective and automatic. If the future is to remain open, then the way the past is lived must be indeterminate.

Refusing Deep Sedimentation

One of the political problems with the lived experience of feminine existence and the way racialized sexual domination is encrusted in the life of the feminine subject is that both actualize through an accumulation of the past that is invisible and forgotten. This process of sedimentation renders the past so dense that it is almost impenetrable, producing the lived experience of racialized heterogender as natural through the very inability to sense its accumulation. Moreover, the density of the past is a heaviness that constrains the field of gendered possibility by weighing down the subject. One's lived experience of gender becomes anchored to a particular style of gender through the heaviness of the past. As Sara Ahmed puts it in her discussion of heteronormativity as an embodied mode of existence, "Through repeating some gestures and not others, or through being orientated in some directions and not others, bodies become contorted: they get twisted into shapes that enable some action *only insofar as they restrict the capacity for other kinds of action*" (2006, 91).

A central insight of accounts of queer temporalities is that breaking from the temporality of normativity to institute an oppositional existence requires and necessitates an open-ended or indeterminate experience and use of time (Sedgwick 1993; Butler 1993; Halberstam 2005; Ahmed 2006). In contrast to the overdetermined temporal structure of normative existence, queer temporalities refuse a temporal orientation that intends to stabilize existence. This indeterminacy institutes and underlies the emancipatory mode of queerness such that a particular relation to and experience of time—how one lives, uses, and is affected by time—is central to the operation of queerness as a politicized refusal of a "normal life." While the queer refusal of normative temporality is often read as a difference between a nonlinear and linear existence, reading this refusal in relation to sedimentation underscores that it is a particular experience of the past that undoes the actualization of normative gendered existence.

In this book, I have emphasized that normative gender is constrained in its possibility to become otherwise because of a particular way the past congeals in a process of deep sedimentation. From a phenomenological perspective, any mode of existence is a result of how the past approaches or touches the present and future such that sedimentation is necessarily central to the actualization of subjectivity and thus to assuming a particular style of existence. Sedimentation allows a subject to concretely have a world. A queer and feminist phenomenology, however, suggests the movement of the past in the sedimentation of normative gendered existence is a distinct kind of movement. Ahmed's queer phenomenology, for instance, points out that heteronormative subjects actualize through the repetition of straight tendencies or lines, which are ways subjects get "stuck in certain alignments as an effect of this work" (2006, 92). What matters in this straight repetition is not the process of sedimentation itself but rather that the repetition intends to get one stuck. The repetition itself, as Butler shows, produces the effect of "real" gender, but that effect, and this is the point I wish to highlight, relies on how the past comes to be lived. The repetition is not superficial and thus at the surface of the present, but is instead a profoundly congealed history. As I argued in chapter 4, it is the deep sediment of normative gender. This deep sedimentation is particular and necessary to the continued operation of systems of domination because it stabilizes the past, preempting individual and collective change and embodied resistance.

On Butler's account, "the anxiously repeated effort" of compulsory norms is "a function of their inefficacy" (1993, 237). The temporality of repetition is thus the operation of the (hetero)norm, which aims to make effective that which is not guaranteed. In turn, Butler proposes that it is the very temporality of repetition that must be engaged to subvert the operation of the norm. Subversion, she claims, relies on "working the weakness in the norm" (237). Queer performativity is, then, about a hyperbolic repetition in order to expose the operation of the norm vis-à-vis temporality. Butler's queer politics of temporality relies on the indeterminacy that remains at the heart of the (overdetermined) habit of heteronormative gender. However, it does not capture the way the operation of the norm aims to render indeterminacy impossible and how this intention is lived. Even as the aim to determine gendered existence always fails, the phenomenological account of normative gender that I have offered in this book suggests that deep sedimentation almost determines the present and future of lived gender, and that this "almost" is lived as a heaviness that jeopardizes the possibility of working the weakness. My point here is not to suggest that a queer politics of subversion cannot destabilize the overdetermination of normativity. Indeed, I take such subversion to be an important strategy of temporal resistance. Rather, I want to suggest that in embodied modes of resistance to normative existence, queer or otherwise, it is necessary to inhabit the past in such a way that it does not weigh one down. The lived past must affect the present and future indeterminately. Since having and living a past allow one to be oriented in the world, the past cannot be so flexible that it refuses itself. Efforts to remember and draw on the past are important political and subjective acts. Thus, it is the way the past moves into and inflects possibility that matters.

A queer relation to the past as indeterminate offers a helpful way to think about what kind of movement of the past is necessary for freedom. If queer orientations challenge "the 'becoming vertical' of ordinary perception," then queering the movement of the past is a way to live time in resistance to gender normativity (Ahmed 2006, 107). Insofar as the temporality of ordinary perception relies on a heavy past that normatively actualizes the present and future, to temporally disrupt normative existence the past must remain malleable. To put it another way, if the temporality of deep sedimentation is a straightening device, a vertical temporal movement that institutes normative existence, then an embodied relation to the past that opens up and renders indeterminate the present and future is to live gender in new ways. Thus, it follows that a habit of indeterminacy is a way to keep open one's relation to time and in turn to challenge the deep sedimentation of normative gender.

This habit of indeterminacy is not about living an indeterminate gender, however. One need not embody or become a gender-fluid subject (though this may be one mode of embodied resistance). Rather, a habit of indeterminacy is about living time and gender in ways that keep open the field of possibility. If normative gender determinations are actually indeterminable, then working the weakness might also mean living the indeterminacy. While Butler's temporal politics of hyperbolic repetition plays on gender's indeterminacy, shifting attention to a habit of indeterminacy allows us to consider how to assume a gendered life—one that may even endure and thus be lived through a sense of determination without the constraints on what gender can be and become.

Silvia Stoller's ethics of indeterminacy gestures toward the cultivation of a habit of indeterminacy as a feminist phenomenological politics. For Stoller, "building awareness with regard to the indeterminacy of gender" makes it "easier to maintain a critical distance from the pre-existing gender norms" (2014, 29). That critical distance, Stoller argues, allows for greater acceptance of nonnormative genders and for the ability for one's own gender to change and for the recognition of the possibility of gender to be otherwise. "Our openness towards this changeability [of gender] implies an *ethics* which recognizes plural gender identities—not only those gender identities which already exist, but a consideration of the possibility of totally unknown identities as well" (30). This habit of indeterminacy is not only a feminist ethics, but, insofar as it intervenes and dismantles the gendered order, is also a phenomenological feminist politics. To stay open to the changeability of gender is thus at once to be able to perceive and affirm a plurality of genders and to undo the grip of structures of domination that refuse this plurality. In calling for the need for habits of indeterminacy, I underscore the need for embodied practices, ways to live and act in the world and with others, ways to actualize a me, that do not require deep sedimentation. The only way to stay open to the changeability of gender is to refuse a deep, almost determinative heaviness to the past. Although the opportunity for change may always be latent in lived gender, the dilemma that habits of normative gender like feminine existence raise are that they paradoxically tend to and aim to sediment determination. A temporal habit that counters this determination, that centers the indeterminacy of the past, is a way to cultivate an openness to gendered existence that does not reify normativity.

Habits of indeterminacy do not suspend sedimentation. They do not deter the individuation of subjectivity or the generation of a particular style of existence. What they do instead is encourage an openness to change and to the capacity to be moved in new ways. But the embodiment of indeterminacy should not be the burden of those who already are most open to change and to those who are used to being moved by others. Habits of indeterminacy are needed most in the lives of those who inhabit the norm.

Reclaiming Time

It is quite difficult to reflect on a resistance effort that is currently under way. Nevertheless, I want to conclude with a brief discussion of what a feminist politics of temporality means in the context of a feminist effort that is calling out the temporal order of sexual domination. In its current form, Time's Up is aimed at fighting the systemic sexual harassment and assault of working women through a legal defense fund, the pursuit of legislation to punish companies that accept harassment and assault, aims to realize gender parity in the workplace, and symbolic declarations of solidarity to women and survivors at high-visibility events and functions. Time figures in here in a few ways. First, there is the calling-out expression—time's up—of being done with being done in. Second, there is the call for women to speak out about what they have endured in the workplace that has been concealed or ignored. Speaking out becomes a way to bring up the past to shift the present and future. Third, there are the efforts to protect and support women that gesture toward a future without systemic sexual domination. All of these efforts have their place in a feminist movement against structures of domination, and indeed, many of them begin to address the temporal modes of resistance I have just discussed.

The primary operation of a phenomenological politics of temporality is to engage and do its work at the level of embodiment, reconfiguring how we are touched by and touch time, how we come to live time in our embodied existence. This affective temporal politics certainly requires changes in the material conditions of existence, but the political demand and the political work must be undertaken in lived experience. A politics of temporality aims to get at the very structures of gendered embodiment to affect it in new, emancipatory ways. Administrative and formal political efforts do not necessarily change the ways gender is lived in the service of power. Visceral practices that sink their teeth in at the prereflective level are crucial to transforming the temporal structures of domination. One must be engaged with one's own use, manipulation, experience, and feeling of time. Moreover, because it is all too possible to change the time of some lives at the expense of others, it is important to remember that the feminist political pursuit of temporality must not neglect the ways the temporal order of sexual domination is predicated on using time against racialized others and those who deviate from gender and sexual norms. Temporal disruption demands a refusal to inherit—that is, to embody—racist, heterosexist constructs and practices. It requires wrestling with the way the racist past moves into the present and future. It requires grappling with the affectiveness of racialized heteronormativity.

Throughout this book, I have focused on the sedimentation of the conspiracy between time and sexual domination in women's lives. The intent of this focus was to give an account of how the contemporary gendered order is deeply rooted in a violent system of racialized sexual domination and to suggest that the foreclosure of liberatory possibilities of gender is achieved through ordinary and state-sanctioned sexual domination against girls and women. Accordingly, I have been preoccupied with the way lived gender is resistant to change, with how the temporal operations of race, gender, and heterosexism refuse feminist worlds, and how one, even as one may live a feminist life, can be hurled into the misogynist world through temporality. I have not focused on feminist, queer, trans, and decolonial practices of resistance to the rigid gendered order I describe, even as I know that such practices are alive, ongoing, and always possible, even in the face of the most severe domination. I have not focused on these resistant modes of existence because the seething presence of the gender norms of racialized heteropatriarchy still thrives. All of our lives continue to be structured by temporalities of domination.

Ultimately, in order for the time of domination to be up, we must pursue different ways to live time. How we live time is a matter of who we can become.

Acknowledgments

It was the labor, wisdom, love, and support of so many that made this book possible.

Bonnie Mann, thank you for being my teacher, for encouraging my philosophical projects, for offering me, and so many others, the intellectual space to grow as feminist thinkers, and for your deep generosity. I am inspired by your philosophical practice and feminist politics, and by your relentless efforts to open up philosophy to those of us who sit in its margins. I would not be where I am without you. Debra Bergoffen, thank you for being the first philosopher to teach me. The time you took with the nineteen-year-old me is etched in my heart, and I remain forever indebted to the countless hours you devoted to my intellectual growth. Dana Rognlie, thank you for your feminist friendship, your philosophical acuity, and for the encouragement and immense labor you invested in this work—it is not lost on me that you have read every draft of every chapter of this book.

I owe a deep thank-you to the faculty in the Department of Philosophy at the University of Oregon with whom I studied. Without a department that intentionally carved out space for feminist thought, I would have never felt comfortable in the world of philosophy. Ted Toadvine took measures beyond expectation to support this work and has seen me through years of writing and navigating the world of academia. I am grateful for the opportunity I had to study with Mark Johnson, Colin Koopman, Scott Pratt, Beata Stawarska, Alejandro Vallega, Daniela Vallega-Neu, Naomi Zack, and Rocío Zambrana. Thank you for being my teachers. Thank you to all the brilliant and kind people I went to graduate school with—you made me a stronger thinker and better person. And many thanks to C. J. Pascoe, whose enthusiasm not only for this work but also for my well-being has been invaluable.

My colleagues from Oklahoma State University, especially Lucy Bailey, Stacy Takacs, and Lawrence Ware—thank you for your guidance, support, and friendship. To all of the undergraduate students in Oklahoma I was fortunate to teach while writing this book, thank you for keeping me alive by showing me what true resilience is, and for your willingness to think and laugh with me in the classroom. You all changed my life, and I would never have finished this book without you.

I am fortunate to have many loved ones who sustained and encouraged me as I wrote and offered love when I was overwhelmed. You know who you are. Thank you for being in my life. And last, deepest thanks to my biological family. I would choose you every day, all day. You not only cared for me throughout the writing of this book, as you have my entire life, but you also made a sincere effort to listen to my ideas. The ways you all seek to hear and understand me just as much as you love me is a true gift.

To all those I have not named, please know you are no less important. My life and this work are anything but individual projects. Thank you.

Notes

Introduction

1. According to one survivor, this is what Roof said during his rampage.
2. Dylan Roof's full confession was recorded on June 18, 2015, by the U.S. Attorney's office. The full confession was made public on December 10, 2016.
3. There was even an interview featuring Roof's black friend (BBC News 2015).
4. Here I'm using Collins's (2000) notion of controlling images. For Collins, stereotypical images are deployed to make systems of domination appear as natural, normal, and inevitable.
5. For instance, although most of the existing data on rape draws attention to the rates of experiences of completed or attempted rapes among (cisgender) women, especially college-age women, the 2015 data released in the "Report on the AAU Campus Climate Survey on Sexual Assault and Sexual Misconduct" (Cantor et al. 2015) suggests that there are higher rates of rape and other forms of sexual violence among LGBTQ+ students on college and university campuses in the United States.
6. Lisa Guenther's critical phenomenology in *Solitary Confinement: Social Death and Its Afterlives* (2013) and Bonnie Mann's feminist phenomenology in *Sovereign Masculinity* (2014) were central texts in the development of my own critical phenomenological approach.
7. With the exception of the important anthology edited by Schües, Olkowski, and Fielding, *Time in Feminist Phenomenology* (2011), feminist phenomenologists have not asked these questions in great detail or in the way I do in this project.
8. There are several discussions of temporality in feminist theory and philosophy that I do not engage in this book. First, Kristeva (1980, 1981, 1985) and Irigaray (1993) also offer accounts of women's relation to time. In particular, they offer positive conceptions of a cyclical temporality of the maternal or feminine subject to recuperate a gendered subjectivity for "woman." Instead of comparing Beauvoir's discussion of temporality with Kristeva's and Irigaray's, I have made a choice to draw attention to Beauvoir's phenomenology of temporality as a framework for accounting for how temporality comes to constrain and confine gendered existence. It's quite possible that there are important connections and points of contention between Beauvoir, Kristeva, and Irigaray on temporality, but I have not prioritized that work in this book. Second, with the exception of the work of Grosz, I have not

engaged discussions of temporality in new materialist feminisms (Braidotti 2002; Barad 2003, 2007; Colebrook 2009) because they are outside the scope of this project.

9. Brownmiller (1975) is one of the most notable feminist thinkers who claims the sexual dimension of the violence of rape is irrelevant to understanding rape.

1. Toward a Feminist Phenomenology of Temporality and Feminine Existence

1. I acknowledge that Beauvoir's phenomenological project in *The Second Sex* is not to account for gender but to account for becoming a woman, and I take it to be important to read Beauvoir's project as a description of woman (*la femme*). Nevertheless, I understand becoming a woman to be, in contemporary terms, the becoming of a gendered subjectivity, and so I use gender not to equate Beauvoir's *la femme* with gender, but to talk about becoming a woman as one kind of gendered subjectivity. McWeeny's (2017) reading of Beauvoir offers an alternative way to understand becoming a woman.

2. There are some exceptions. Mann (2008, 2014) draws attention to Beauvoir's continual address of the theme of temporality. Deutscher (2008) also offers a sharp and elaborate analysis of temporality in relation to Beauvoir's account of gendered labor. This is also not to say that Beauvoir scholars have not engaged temporality in relation to Beauvoir's work at all (Tidd 2011; Miller 2012). Rather, my point is that the discussion of how a woman lives time in volume 2 of *The Second Sex* has not received significant attention as a central feature of her descriptive account.

3. I use the 2010 English translation of *The Second Sex*. When I translate the original text differently, I use my own translation of the original French edition. Elsewhere I discuss the philosophical difference between the Parshley translation and Borde and Malovany-Chevallier's recent translation of the famous sentence, and justify my agreement with the Parshley translation regarding this sentence (Burke 2017).

4. Heinämaa (1997) points out that Butler's readings of Beauvoir's conception of the body are inconsistent. Although I agree with Heinämaa on this point, it seems apparent to me that Butler is quite consistent in reading "becoming" as the temporality of gender in *The Second Sex*.

5. Heinämaa (2003) traces the concept of style from Husserl to Merleau-Ponty to Beauvoir, arguing that style helps show that sexual difference is neither voluntary nor determined. Mann offers an account of gender as style that underscores gender as "ontological weight in the body" (2014, 83). On Mann's account, a phenomenological account of gender as style edifies our understanding of why gender comes to matter so much to who we are, how we act, what we look like, how we feel, and how we are perceived by others because it pays careful attention to the aesthetic dimension of gender.

6. Feminist readers of Beauvoir often draw comparisons between Merleau-Ponty and Beauvoir, suggesting that the two phenomenologists deploy phenomenological concepts in similar ways. For instance, Heinämaa (2003) insists that Beauvoir is up to much of what Merleau-Ponty is in his work. Tidd (1999) even underscores the relation between Merleau-Ponty's and Beauvoir's accounts of temporality and embodiment.

7. Among Beauvoir scholars, there is little agreement on how to understand immanence and transcendence. The most dominant understandings of immanence and transcendence suggest that they ought to be read as either existentialist notions or as Marxist–Hegelian ones, but not first and foremost as temporal categories (Lloyd 1984; Le Doeuff 1987; Kruks 1995, 1998; Arp 2001; Lundgren-Gothlin 1996; Veltman 2006; Deutscher 2008; Moi 2008). Deutscher's (2008) work is an exception. Following Marx, Deutscher claims that Beauvoir associates repetition with the immanent domain insofar as it is labor that perpetuates life, while transcendence is a creative, future-oriented temporality that materializes human existence as more than mere animality. I am sympathetic to Deutscher's reading insofar as it underscores immanence and transcendence as modes of temporality. Nevertheless, I think a phenomenological account of immanence and transcendence provides a more robust and embodied account of the relation between temporality and gendered subjectivity. Although Deutscher mentions that Beauvoir's account of repetition is a result of drawing "on a crowd of interpretive and philosophical models" (108), the majority of Deutscher's account of repetition in *The Second Sex* claims that Beauvoir echoes and expands on Marx.

8. In contrast to my reading, McWeeny (2017) suggests the rupture is the temporal constitution of a woman's existence.

9. Some of the women in Beauvoir's novels settle into temporalities that seem to complicate this point. For instance, in *The Mandarins* (1955), Paule's endless devotion to Henri confines her to the time of their relationship, which, in the context of the novel, is the past. However, Paule's refusal to move on with her life and her demand to maintain what once was with Henri is a way to maintain and thus repeat her existence as *for* Henri. For this reason, her past can be read as a past made into a passive present.

2. Sexualized Racism and the Politics of Time

1. Deer (2015) offers an important discussion of how and whether American Indian victims of rape are the exception to this reality.

2. Draz (2017) offers an insightful account of how the state wields the coloniality of gender vis-à-vis temporality to maintain normative gender formations by rendering some transgender identities valid and others invalid. For Draz, and I

agree, there is thus good reason to be suspicious of appealing to the origin story of "sex" insofar as it has a colonial history.

3. This provides an important analysis of colonialism and race to Butler's ([1990] 1999) claim about the norms of intelligibility that regulate what counts as acceptable gender. While she points out schemas of intelligibility produce the norms of recognition that confer human status, she does not account for the racialization of the schemas of intelligibility.

4. Importantly, this point is reminiscent of Butler's (1993) notion of the specters of the abject—the queer figures who are at once constitutively outside and inside normative gender formations. Here, however, the specters of normative gender are the colonized.

5. Maldonado-Torres's (2007) critical reading of Heidegger's account of the meaning of human existence as being in time, an existence that is thrown toward the future, offers a way to extend Holland's (2012) insight and claim that existing in time is an impossibility for the colonized subject in a racist milieu.

3. Beware of Strangers!

1. Several large newspapers in the United States transcribed the speech. Copies of prepared remarks were provided to the press but were allegedly very different from Trump's delivered remarks (*Washington Post* 2015).

2. Almost a century before Davis, antilynching activist, journalist, and black feminist Ida B. Wells (1892) exposed the myth in her pamphlet, "Southern Horrors: Lynch Law in All Its Phases." Moreover, decades after Wells and before Davis, American philosopher and critical race theorist W. E. B. Du Bois also pointed out the significance of the false charge of rape created by white America: "The charge of rape against Colored Americans was invented by the white South after Reconstruction to excuse mob violence" ([1919], 1983, 193).

3. The particular image of the vulnerable feminine (white) woman central to this white rape mythology has surfaced in antitransgender bathroom bill legislation. Such legislation is predicated on the belief that cisgender and gender-conforming girls and women must be protected from a predatory "man in a dress." While this image of transgender women is transphobia par excellence, a representation and belief that trans women are not real women (Bettcher 2007), the image of the sexually violable woman has historically surfaced as the image of the vulnerable white woman. So although the transphobic rape mythology emerges as a social and political mechanism of control that is specific to producing ontological and physical violence against trans people, the myth itself is not entirely new. Moreover, that the racial desegregation of public bathrooms in particular set off a national white panic regarding the safety and sexual health of white women underscores the racialized history of bathroom panics in the United States. That the

logic of the myth of the black male rapist motivates and rationalizes the marginalization and criminalization of transgender people through the reconstruction of "white woman" as vulnerable to rape only attests to the power of the myth and its central role in the production and maintenance of the gendered social order.

4. Feminist scholar of masculinity and violence against women Jackson Katz implies this connection when he writes, "White girls learn from an early age . . . that the real danger lurks with dark-skinned predators," a message "many white women continue to take . . . to heart" (2006, 135). He does not, however, give an explicit account of the connection between the myths.

5. In their popular book on unconscious bias, *Blindspot*, psychologists Mahzarin R. Banaji and Anthony G. Greenwald refer to "ingrained habits of thought that lead to errors in how we perceive, remember, reason, and make decisions" as mindbugs (2016, 4). On their account, cognitive operations—"the mind"—rely on automatic associations, which come to be habitual and patterned ways of thinking, or mindbugs. One of the most powerful types of mindbugs are social mindbugs, habitual ways of thinking about and making decisions about people that often generate false feelings about who people are, and in so doing serve as weak justification for action toward a particular person or group of people. Importantly, social mindbugs are a product of social habits of thinking and acting. However, discussions and research on unconscious bias suggest that cognitive bias does not lead to bias in behavior. But the phenomenological view of prereflective habits provides a different way to address how social and historical processes of dehumanization and systems of power produce both unconscious bias and behavior. From a phenomenological perspective, the habituation or sedimentation of such processes and systems are structures of perception, which means they impact not how we think but rather how we feel and relate to the world and to others. As such, we don't just hold biases in our minds; we also hold them and live them in our bodily existence with others. As affective and bodily, accordingly, it is not necessarily possible to measure all operations of bias.

6. I want to be clear that I do not condone carceral logic, but I am concerned with the way white cisgender heterosexual middle- and upper-class men like Turner are never subject to incarceration in ways that other people are.

7. I gather that white girls are receiving this cautionary lesson about strangers in ways that girls of other racial and ethnic groups are not—and, I presume, with more intensity. However, Phillips's (2000) work also suggests that young women of various racial and ethnic groups receive stranger danger warnings. Given that white supremacy is a structure of social order rather than mere acts of whites against people of color, the mutation of the myth of the black male rapist into the myth of stranger rape underscores the circulation of white supremacy and a larger cultural incompetency around the reality of rape.

8. In other work, I offer a reading of Beauvoir's account of "becoming a woman" that is different than Bergoffen's reading of the relation between *a* woman/Woman. For Bergoffen (2017), the "famous sentence" of volume 2 of *The Second Sex* attends to the reality of becoming Woman as a woman such that the sentence, when translated into English, should read, "One is not born, but rather becomes (a) woman." Here I follow Bergoffen's reading of Beauvoir's understanding of how women are made Woman. I (Burke 2017) still claim the translated sentence should read, as Parshley (1953) translated it, "One is not born, but rather becomes a woman." It is still my view that the explicit inclusion of the indefinite article underscores Beauvoir's phenomenological commitment to becoming.

4. Anonymity and the Temporality of Normative Gender

1. Stoller's work (2009, 2010, 2014) bridging the poststructuralist and phenomenological divide has been influential to my own reading of temporality in these allegedly disparate traditions.

2. Feminist phenomenologists have been doing such recuperative work as a response to Butler's work and the poststructuralist tradition for some time now (Alcoff 2000; Kruks 2001; Mann 2006, 2017).

3. Butler does not explicitly account for what philosophical sources motivate and inspire her use and understanding of sedimentation. It is tempting to attribute the concept to Foucault's and Nietzsche's influence on her work. I have resisted such attribution here. It is quite possible that this is a particularly Butlerian notion of sedimentation that need not be attributed to "founding fathers" of Continental philosophy. However, I do not deny that it would be an interesting history of philosophy project to tease out the overlaps and distinctions. I have hesitated to do so here as a way to resist the urge and norm to read feminist philosophers as only borrowing concepts from (white) men.

4. Sullivan (2001) offers an extensive account of gender as habit. Although Sullivan draws on discussions of habit in American philosophy, primarily those of John Dewey as well as those of Merleau-Ponty and Butler, I have not engaged her account here. Because I am particularly interested in the connection between habit and anonymity in relation to Merleau-Ponty's work as a resource for a feminist phenomenology of gender, I find Sullivan's positive reconstruction of habit to exceed this scope. However, Sullivan's critique of Merleau-Ponty's notion of anonymity is at odds with my reading, and therefore there is a point of contention between our own conceptions of habit.

5. Although Merleau-Ponty later distances himself from the emphasis on a constituting consciousness found in *Phenomenology of Perception* (2012), which admits to a metaphysics of presence to some degree, the *Phenomenology* also begins to

break with the primacy of the present and self-presence through the notion of anonymity.

6. I also believe this historical feminist suspicion of gender neutrality has a limit. In more recent years, there are gender-nonconforming, nonbinary, and/or trans individuals who make claims to genderless, agender, or gender-neutral identities and lives. I do not believe these are, as Halberstam (2018) has suggested, whimsical and untenable claims. I think it is both necessary and possible to be suspicious of patriarchal gender neutrality and affirmative of trans conceptions of gender neutrality.

7. Within the context of the *Phenomenology of Perception*, Merleau-Ponty's (2012) account of anonymity emphasizes its relation to the habit body such that anonymity underscores the temporal dimension of sedimentation, but elsewhere he prioritizes an excessive dimension of anonymity. This excessive dimension of anonymity is underscored much more in his later work. For instance, in "Eye and Mind," he accounts for "an imaginary texture of the real" that opens up and generates new expressions of reality (1993, 126). Here the imaginary is the anonymous, invisible dimension of the present reality.

5. Specters of Violence

1. Madriz notes that the fear of crime in general circumscribes and controls women's lives: "The fear of crime is one of the most oppressive and deceitful sources of informal control of women" (1997, 343). The fear of rape is one of the most central, and because of its prevalence most pernicious, expressions of this fear in women's lives.

2. Murphy offers an important provocation regarding the place of violence in the philosophical imaginary: "The images of violence that figure with such prominence in contemporary theory are important to consider . . . since the philosophical imaginary profoundly . . . shapes our affective response to the world; it informs what we fear and hope, herald and condemn" (2012, 2). Murphy wonders what the pervasive motif of violence does to philosophy and to a philosopher's capacities for seeing, thinking, and feeling otherwise. I take seriously that a continued focus on violence in the feminist imaginary can operate as a constraint on how gender materializes and limits the imagination. However, my account of spectral violence aims to destabilize the centrality of violence in order to open up the imagination rather than shut it down.

3. The way the threat of rape haunts and the intensity of this haunting will undoubtedly vary depending on one's social location, including one's gender assignment at birth, socioeconomic status, race, sexuality, bodily capacities, and nationality.

4. I take this to also suggest that there is an underdeveloped commitment to materiality in Butler's work that has been largely criticized for its absence. See Mann (2006) for a sustained criticism of Butler's notion of the constitutive outside in relation to the question of materiality.

5. Interestingly, in an interview, Butler suggests that she departs from Foucault and is more closely aligned with Derrida on the very question of what "there is": "But I also want to claim that the ontological claim can never capture its object, and this view makes me somewhat different from Foucault and aligns me temporarily with the Kantian tradition as it has been taken up by Derrida" (1998, 279). Butler continues, though briefly, to suggest that her claims to what "there is" is a gesture toward what cannot be captured. I understand this gesture to in some way relate to Derrida's notion of hauntology.

6. Pascoe (2007) draws attention to the specter as a populated zone of social life in her discussion of one student, Ricky, who is the fag not only because of his sexuality but also as a result of his nonnormative gender identification and presentation. For Ricky, existing as fag, rather than alongside the threat of becoming a fag, made his life at River High unlivable.

7. For Spivak, Derrida presents a how-to-mourn-your-father book in his analysis of the haunting of communism. "Woman is nowhere," she writes (1995, 66). Spivak demands that we take seriously how even Derrida's critique of ontology is always already haunted by its exclusion of women, and subaltern women in particular.

8. Heidegger (1962) argues that mood is a necessary affective dimension of experience. Without a mood, or affective atmosphere to existence, we would not have a sense of, or be able to make sense of, the self and the world.

9. This claim is not meant to suggest that the specter only produces and works through feminine women or girls. Perhaps its telos is to do so, but the specter of rape also lurks over the lives of nonconforming and transgender women and girls as either might police them into intelligibility or punish them for failing to (be able to) conform to white standards of feminine existence.

10. A host of contemporary television shows, especially *The Killing* (2011–14) and *The Fall* (2013–16), depict the danger and pleasure of the specter of rape quite well. In fact, in *The Fall*, the lurking and titillating rapist is aptly named Paul Spector.

11. I am also sure that some men, nonbinary, and agender people also endure spectral violence, and even the specter of rape, but what that looks or feels like, as well as the historical and material conditions of its production, are beyond my scope here. Ableson (2016) offers a sociological account of spectral violence in trans men's lives.

12. Heidegger (1962) understands care as the basis for our existence. Care is an external condition and internal condition that allows for existence. He suggests that the structure of care is an open relation between the past, present, and future.

13. Szymanski and Balsam (2011) offer a specific example of the way heterosexist domination manifests as trauma in women's lives.

14. Freedman's (2014) philosophical memoir about surviving rape also attests to this double bind.

15. Furthermore, Heyes's (2016) phenomenology of the rape of women who are unconscious suggests that regaining a relation to the future is distinctly difficult for girls and women who are raped while unconscious or semiconscious. According to Heyes, survivors of rapes of this kind lose the ability to retreat to sleep, a realm Merleau-Ponty associates with the dimension of anonymity that is necessary to having personal time.

6. Feminist Politics and the Difference of Time

1. Though, arguably, the Time's Up campaign began two months earlier in November 2017 when *Time* magazine published an open letter from the Alianza Nacional de Campesinas regarding sexual harassment and assault. Hollywood's organizing of Time's Up did not neglect to recognize the open letter, but it is worthwhile to note that Time's Up was spurred by the organizing efforts of working-class women of color.

2. Similar to the visibility of Time's Up, although the hashtag campaign was popularized by Hollywood celebrity Alyssa Milano, the Me Too movement began in 2006 with civil rights and feminist activist Tarana Burke. The initial erasure of Burke in the Me Too movement is just one way contemporary feminist resistance efforts continue to be structured by whiteness and struggle to undermine this structuring.

3. I am referring to the activist work of women such as Annie Clark, Andrea Pino, and Sofie Karasek, who inspired, in part, the Obama administration's investigation into sexual assault on college campuses, started the organization End Rape on Campus, and were featured in the documentary *The Hunting Ground* (2015).

4. I borrow the language of fracturing from Al-Saji's (2014) account of hesitation.

5. I have argued elsewhere in this book that feminine existence can be imposed in a particular moment even if one does not have a personal habit of feminine existence. The habit of feminine existence should thus be understood as at once social and individual. Here I refer to subjects who embody this habit. I gather that those who have not been done in by (or try to undo being done in by) this habit already live an event of delay.

6. As Deutscher (2008) points out, although Beauvoir tends to view repetition as negative, she also does not condemn housework in itself. Rather, Beauvoir is concerned with the conditions of the labor. The repetitive character of the

housewife's efforts is a problem insofar as she has been relegated to such work and that such work cannot confer her own future. The domestic activity might institute a present, but the future still belongs to a man.

7. I am thinking in particular about the so-called protective custody of solitary confinement that trans prisoners are subjected to as a result of their gendered existence.

Bibliography

Ableson, Miriam. 2016. "Negotiating Vulnerability and Fear: Rethinking the Relationship between Violence and Contemporary Masculinity." In *Exploring Masculinities: Identity, Inequality, Continuity, and Change*, edited by C. J. Pascoe and Tristan Bridges, 394–401. Oxford: Oxford University Press.

Ahmed, Sara. 2000. *Strange Encounters: Embodied Others in Postcoloniality*. New York: Routledge.

Ahmed, Sara. 2004. *The Cultural Politics of Emotion*. New York: Routledge.

Ahmed, Sara. 2006. *Queer Phenomenology: Orientations, Objects, Others*. Durham, N.C.: Duke University Press.

Alcoff, Linda Martín. 2000. "Phenomenology, Post-structuralism, and Feminist Theory on the Concept of Experience." In *Feminist Phenomenology*, edited by Linda Fischer and Lester Embree, 39–56. Dordrecht: Kluwer Academic.

Alcoff, Linda Martín. 2005. *Visible Identities: Race, Gender, and the Self*. Oxford: Oxford University Press.

Al-Saji, Alia. 2008. "'A Past Which Has Never Been Present': Bergsonian Dimensions in Merleau-Ponty's *Theory of the Prepersonal*." *Research in Phenomenology* 38 (1): 41–71.

Al-Saji, Alia. 2013. "Too Late: Racialized Time and the Closure of the Past." *Insights* 6 (5): 2–13.

Al-Saji, Alia. 2014. "A Phenomenology of Hesitation: Interrupting Racializing Habits of Seeing." In *Living Alterities: Phenomenology, Embodiment, and Race*, edited by Emily Lee, 133–72. Albany: State University of New York Press.

Arp, Kristana. 2001. *The Bonds of Freedom: Simone de Beauvoir's Existentialist Ethics*. Chicago: Carus.

Baldwin, James. 1953. "Stranger in the Village." *Harper's Magazine*, October 1953, 42–48.

Banaji, Mahzarin, and Anthony Greenwald. 2016. *Blindspot: Hidden Biases of Good People*. New York: Bantam.

Barad, Karen. 2003. "Posthumanist Performativity: Toward an Understanding of How Matter Comes to Matter." *Signs* 28 (3): 801–31.

Barad, Karen. 2007. *Meeting the Universe Halfway: Quantum Physics and the Entanglement of Matter and Meaning*. Durham, N.C.: Duke University Press.

Barthes, Roland. 1972. *Mythologies*. Translated by Annette Lavers. New York: Noonday Press.

Bartky, Sandra. 1990. *Femininity and Domination: Studies in the Phenomenology of Oppression*. New York: Routledge.

BBC News. 2015. "Dylan Roof's Black Friend Speaks Out: 'He Never Said Anything Racist.'" BBC News, June 20, 2015. https://www.bbc.com/.

Beauvoir, Simone de. 1949. *Le Deuxième Sexe I et II*. Paris: Gallimard.

Beauvoir, Simone de. 1955. *The Mandarins*. Translated by Leonard M. Friedman. New York: Norton.

Beauvoir, Simone de. 1976. *The Ethics of Ambiguity*. Translated by Bernard Frechtman. New York: Citadel Press.

Beauvoir, Simone de. 2005. "Pyrrhus and Cineas." In *Simone de Beauvoir: Philosophical Writings*, edited by Margaret Simons, 89–149. Champaign: University of Illinois Press.

Beauvoir, Simone de. 2010. *The Second Sex*. Translated by Constance Borde and Sheila Malovany-Chevallier. New York: Knopf.

Bederman, Gail. 1996. *Manliness and Civilization: A Cultural History of Gender and Race in the United States, 1800–1917*. Chicago: University of Chicago Press.

Benbow, Mark E. 2010. "Birth of a Quotation: Woodrow Wilson and 'Like Writing History with Lightning.'" In *Journal of the Gilded Age and Progressive Era* 9 (4): 509–33.

Bergoffen, Debra. 2002. "Simone de Beauvoir and Jean-Paul Sartre: Woman, Man, and the Desire of God." *Constellations* 9 (3): 409–18.

Bergoffen, Debra. 2017. "The Floating 'a.'" In *On Ne Naît Pas Femme: On Le Devient: The Life of a Sentence*, edited by Bonnie Mann and Martina Ferrari, 143–58. Oxford: Oxford University Press.

Bergson, Henri. (1889) 2001. *Time and Free Will: An Essay on the Immediate Data of Consciousness*. Translated by F. L. Pogson. New York: Dover.

Bergson, Henri. (1896) 1990. *Matter and Memory*. Translated by Nancy Margaret Paul and W. Scott Palmer. New York: Zone Books.

Bettcher, Talia Mae. 2006. "Understanding Transphobia: Authenticity and Sexual Violence." In *Trans/Forming Feminisms: Trans-Feminist Voices Speak Out*, edited by Krista Scott-Dixon, 203–10. Toronto: Sumach Press.

Bettcher, Talia Mae. 2007. "Evil Deceivers and Make-Believers: On Transphobic Violence and the Politics of Illusion." *Hypatia* 22 (3): 43–65.

Braidotti, Rosi. 2002. *Metamorphoses: Towards a Materialist Theory of Becoming*. Cambridge: Polity Press.

Brandes, Heidi. 2015. "Ex-Oklahoma Policeman Preyed on Women 'No One Cared About': Prosecutors." Reuters, December 7, 2015. https://www.reuters.com/.

Brison, Susan. 2002. *Aftermath, Violence, and the Remaking of a Self*. Princeton, N.J.: Princeton University Press.

Brown, Wendy. 2001. *Politics Out of History*. Princeton, N.J.: Princeton University Press.

Brownmiller, Susan. 1975. *Against Our Will: Men, Women, and Rape*. New York: Random House.

Burke, Megan. 2013. "Anonymous Temporality and Gender: Re-reading Merleau-Ponty." *philoSOPHIA* 3 (2): 138–57.

Burke, Megan. 2017. "Becoming *a* Woman: Reading Beauvoir's Response to the Woman Question." In *On Ne Naît Pas Femme: On Le Devient: The Life of a Sentence*, edited by Bonnie Mann and Martina Ferrari, 159–74. Oxford: Oxford University Press.

Burstow, Bonnie. 2003. "Toward a Radical Understanding of Trauma and Trauma Work." *Violence against Women* 9 (11): 1293–317.

Butler, Judith. 1986. "Sex and Gender in Simone de Beauvoir's *Second Sex*." *Yale French Studies* 72:35–49.

Butler, Judith. 1988. "Performative Acts and Gender Constitution: An Essay in Phenomenology and Feminist Theory." *Theatre Journal* 40 (4): 519–31.

Butler, Judith. (1990) 1999. *Gender Trouble: Feminism and the Subversion of Identity*. 2nd ed. New York: Routledge Classics.

Butler, Judith. 1993. *Bodies That Matter: On the Discursive Limits of "Sex."* New York: Routledge.

Butler, Judith. 1995. "Contingent Foundations: Feminism and the Question of Postmodernism." In *Feminist Contentions: A Philosophical Exchange*, edited by Seyla Benhabib, Judith Butler, Drucilla Cornell, and Nancy Fraser, 1–21. New York: Routledge.

Butler, Judith. 1997. *The Psychic Life of Power: Theories in Subjection*. Stanford, Calif.: Stanford University Press.

Butler, Judith. 1998. "How Bodies Come to Matter: An Interview with Judith Butler." Conducted by Irene Costera Meijer and Baukje Prins. *Signs* 23 (2): 275–86.

Cahill, Ann. 2001. *Rethinking Rape*. Ithaca, N.Y.: Cornell University Press.

Cahill, Ann. 2009. "In Defense of Self-Defense." *Philosophical Papers* 38 (3): 363–80.

Cahill, Ann, and Grayson Hunt. 2016. "Should Feminists Defend Self-Defense?" *International Journal of Feminist Approaches to Bioethics* 9 (2): 172–82.

Cantor, David, Bonnie Fisher, Susan Chibnell, et al. 2015. "Report on the AAU Campus Climate Survey on Sexual Assault and Sexual Misconduct." Association of American Universities, September 21, 2015. https://www.aau.edu/sites/default/files/%40%20Files/Climate%20Survey/AAU_Campus_Climate_Survey_12_14_15.pdf.

Casey, Edward. 2000. *Remembering: A Phenomenological Study*. 2nd ed. Bloomington: Indiana University Press.

Colebrook, Claire. 2009. "Stratigraphic Time, Women's Time." *Australian Feminist Studies* 24 (59): 11–16.

Collins, Patricia Hill. 2000. *Black Feminist Thought: Knowledge, Consciousness, and the Politics of Empowerment*. 2nd ed. New York: Routledge.

Collins, Patricia Hill. 2004. *Black Sexual Politics: African Americans, Gender, and the New Racism*. New York: Routledge.

Cooper, Brittney. 2016. "The Racial Politics of Time" (video filmed October 2016 in San Francisco, Calif.). TEDWomen, https://www.ted.com/talks/brittney_cooper_the_racial_politics_of_time.

Cornell, Drucilla. 1995. *The Imaginary Domain: Abortion, Pornography, and Sexual Harassment*. New York: Routledge.

Crenshaw, Kimberlé. 1991. "Mapping the Margins: Intersectionality, Identity Politics, and Violence against Women of Color." *Stanford Law Review* 43 (6): 1241–99.

Davis, Angela. 1981. *Women, Race, and Class*. New York: Random House.

Deer, Sarah. 2015. *The Beginning and End of Rape: Confronting Sexual Violence in Native America*. Minneapolis: University of Minnesota Press.

Derrida, Jacques. 1973. *Speech and Phenomena and Other Essays on Husserl's "Theory of Signs."* Translated by David B. Allison. Evanston, Ill.: Northwestern University Press.

Derrida, Jacques. 1982. "Ousia and Grammē: Note on a Note from *Being and Time*." In *Margins of Philosophy*, translated by Alan Bass, 29–67. Chicago: University of Chicago Press.

Derrida, Jacques. 1994. *Specters of Marx*. Translated by Peggy Kamuf. New York: Routledge.

Derrida, Jacques, and Bernard Steigler. 2002. "Spectrographies." In *Echographies of Television: Filmed Interviews*, translated by Jennifer Bajor, 113–34. Cambridge: Polity Press.

Deutscher, Penelope. 2008. *The Philosophy of Simone de Beauvoir: Ambiguity, Conversion, Resistance*. New York: Cambridge University Press.

Dinshaw, Carolyn, Lee Edelman, Roderick A. Ferguson, et al. 2007. "Theorizing Queer Temporalities: A Roundtable Discussion." *GLQ: A Journal of Gay and Lesbian Studies* 13 (2–3): 177–95.

Draz, Marie. 2017. "Born This Way? Time and the Coloniality of Gender." *Journal of Speculative Philosophy* 31 (3): 372–84.

Du Bois, W. E. B. (1919) 1983. "Rape." In *Selections from the Crisis*. White Plains, N.Y.: Kraus-Thomson.

Essed, Philomena. 1991. *Understanding Everyday Racism: An Interdisciplinary Theory*. Thousand Oaks, Calif.: Sage.

Falcón, Sylvanna. 2001. "Rape as a Weapon of War: Advancing Human Rights for Women at the U.S.–Mexico Border." *Social Justice* 28 (2): 31–50.

Fanon, Frantz. 1967. *Black Skin, White Masks*. Translated by Charles Lam Markmann. New York: Grove Press.

Fausto-Sterling, Anne. 2000. *Sexing the Body: Gender Politics and the Construction of Sexuality*. New York: Basic Books.

Ferguson, Roderick. 2003. *Aberrations in Black: Toward a Queer of Color Critique*. Minneapolis: University of Minnesota Press.

Ferguson, Roderick. 2005. "Of Our Normative Strivings: African American Studies and the Histories of Sexuality." *Social Text* 23 (3–4): 85–100.

Ferraro, Kenneth. 1996. "Women's Fear of Victimization: Shadow of Sexual Assault?" *Social Forces* 75 (2): 667–90.

Fisher, Linda. 2011. "Gendering Embodied Memory." In *Time in Feminist Phenomenology*, edited by Christina Schües, Dorothea E. Olkowski, and Helen A. Fielding, 91–110. Bloomington: Indiana University Press.

Freccero, Carla. 2006. *Queer/Early/Modern*. Durham, N.C.: Duke University Press.

Freccero, Carla. 2007. "Queer Spectrality: Haunting the Past." In *A Companion to Lesbian, Gay, Bisexual, Transgender, and Queer Studies*, edited by George E. Haggerty and Molly McGarry, 194–213. Malden, Mass.: Blackwell.

Freedman, Estelle. 2015. *Redefining Rape: Sexual Violence in the Era of Suffrage and Segregation*. Cambridge, Mass.: Harvard University Press.

Freedman, Karyn. 2014. *One Hour in Paris: A True Story of Rape and Recovery*. Chicago: University of Chicago Press.

Freeman, Elizabeth. 2010. *Time Binds: Queer Temporalities, Queer Histories*. Durham, N.C.: Duke University Press.

Gatens, Moira. 1995. *Imaginary Bodies: Ethics, Power, and Corporeality*. New York: Routledge.

Gordon, Avery. 1997a. *Ghostly Matters: Haunting and the Sociological Imagination*. Minneapolis: University of Minnesota Press.

Gordon, Lewis. 1997b. *Her Majesty's Other Children: Sketches of Racism from a Neocolonial Age*. Lanham, Md.: Rowman & Littlefield.

Gordon, Margaret, and Stephanie Riger. 1989. *The Female Fear*. New York: Free Press.

Griffin, Susan. (1971) 1989. "Rape: The All-American Crime." In *Feminism and Philosophy*, edited by Mary Vetterling-Braggin, Frederick Elliston, and Jane English, 313–32. Totowa, N.J.: Rowman & Littlefield.

Grosz, Elizabeth. 1994. *Volatile Bodies: Toward a Corporeal Feminism*. Indianapolis: Indiana University Press.

Grosz, Elizabeth. 2004. *Nick of Time: Politics, Evolution, and the Untimely*. Durham, N.C.: Duke University Press.

Grosz, Elizabeth. 2005. *Time Travels: Feminism, Nature, Power*. Durham, N.C.: Duke University Press, 2005.

Guenther, Lisa. 2013. *Solitary Confinement: Social Death and Its Afterlives*. Minneapolis: University of Minnesota Press.

Gunn Allen, Paula. 1986. *The Sacred Hoop: Recovering the Feminine in American Indian Traditions*. Boston: Beacon Press.

Halberstam, Jack. 2005. *In a Queer Time and Place: Transgender Bodies, Subcultural Lives*. New York: New York University Press, 2005.

Halberstam, Jack. 2018. *Trans*: A Quick and Quirky Account of Gender Variability*. Berkeley: University of California Press.

Haraway, Donna. 1991. *Simians, Cyborgs, and Women: The Reinvention of Nature*. New York: Routledge.

Heidegger, Martin. 1962. *Being and Time*. Translated by John Macquarrie and Edward Robinson. New York: Harper & Row.

Heinämaa, Sara. 1996. "Woman—Nature, Product, Style? Rethinking the Foundations of Feminist Philosophy of Science." In *Feminism, Science, and the Philosophy of Science*, edited by Lynn Hankinson Nelson and Jack Nelson, 289–308. Dordrecht: Kluwer Academic.

Heinämaa, Sara. 1997. "What Is a Woman? Butler and Beauvoir on the Foundations of the Sexual Difference." *Hypatia* 12 (1): 20–39.

Heinämaa, Sara. 2003. *Toward a Phenomenology of Sexual Difference: Husserl, Merleau-Ponty, Beauvoir*. New York: Rowman & Littlefield.

Herman, Judith. 1992. *Trauma and Recovery: The Aftermath of Violence—From Domestic Abuse to Political Terror*. New York: Basic Books.

Heyes, Cressida. 2016. "Dead to the World: Rape, Unconsciousness, and Social Media." *Signs* 41 (2): 361–83.

Hlavka, Heather. 2014. "Normalizing Sexual Violence: Young Women Account for Harassment and Abuse." *Gender and Society* 28 (3): 337–58.

Holland, Sharon Patricia. 2012. *The Erotic Life of Racism*. Durham, N.C.: Duke University Press.

Hollander, Jocelyn. 2001. "Vulnerability and Dangerousness: The Construction of Gender through Conversations about Violence." *Gender and Society* 15 (1): 83–109.

Hollander, Jocelyn. 2004. "'I Can Take Care of Myself': The Impact of Self-Defense Training on Women's Lives." *Violence against Women* 10 (3): 205–35.

Hollander, Jocelyn. 2014. "Does Self-Defense Training Prevent Sexual Violence against Women?" *Violence against Women* 20 (3): 252–69.

hooks, bell. 1981. *Ain't I a Woman: Black Women and Feminism*. Boston: South End Press.

Husserl, Edmund. 1991. *On the Phenomenology of the Consciousness of Internal Time (1893–1917)*. Translated by John Barnett Brough. Dordrecht: Kluwer Academic.

Irigaray, Luce. 1993. *An Ethics of Sexual Difference*. Translated by Carolyn Burke and Gillian C. Gill. Ithaca, N.Y.: Cornell University Press.

Jones, Janine. 2013. "If You See Something, Say Something." *Black Scholar* 43 (4): 59–64.

Katz, Jackson. 2006. *The Macho Paradox: Why Some Men Hurt Women and How All Men Can Help.* Naperville, Ill.: Sourcebooks.

Kristeva, Julia. 1980. *Desire in Language: A Semiotic Approach to Art and Literature.* Translated by Thomas Gora and Alice Jardine. New York: Columbia University Press.

Kristeva, Julia. 1981. "Women's Time." Translated by Alice Jardine and Harry Blake. *Signs* 7 (1): 13–35.

Kristeva, Julia. 1985. "Stabat Mater." Translated by Arthur Goldhammer. *Poetics Today* 6 (102): 133–52.

Kruks, Sonia. 1995. "Teaching Sartre about Freedom." In *Feminist Interpretations of Simone de Beauvoir,* edited by Margaret Simons, 79–96. University Park: Pennsylvania State University Press.

Kruks, Sonia. 1998. "Beauvoir: The Weight of the Situation." In *Simone de Beauvoir: A Critical Reader,* edited by Elizabeth Fallaize, 43–71. New York: Routledge.

Kruks, Sonia. 2001. *Retrieving Experience: Subjectivity and Recognition in Feminist Politics.* Ithaca, N.Y.: Cornell University Press.

Le Doeuff, Michèle. 1987. "Operative Philosophy: Simone de Beauvoir and Existentialism." In *Critical Essays on Simone de Beauvoir,* edited by Elaine Marks, 144–53. Boston: Hall.

Lee, Michelle Ye Hee. 2015. "Donald Trump's False Comments Connecting Mexican Immigrants and Crime." *Washington Post,* July 8, 2015. https://www.washingtonpost.com/.

Lloyd, Genevieve. 1984. *The Man of Reason: "Male" and "Female" in Western Philosophy.* York: Methuen.

Luciano, Dana. 2007. *Arranging Grief: Sacred Time and the Body in Nineteenth-Century America.* New York: New York University Press.

Lugones, María. 2007. "Heterosexualism and the Colonial/Modern Gender System." *Hypatia* 22 (1): 186–219.

Lugones, María. 2010. "Toward a Decolonial Feminism." *Hypatia* 25 (4): 742–59.

Lundgren-Gothlin, Eva. 1996. *Sex and Existence: Simone de Beauvoir's "The Second Sex."* Translated by Linda Schenck. London: Athlone Press.

MacKinnon, Catharine. 1979. *The Sexual Harassment of Working Women: A Case of Sex Discrimination.* New Haven, Conn.: Yale University Press.

MacKinnon, Catharine. 1988. *Feminism Unmodified: Discourses on Life and Law.* Cambridge, Mass.: Harvard University Press.

MacKinnon, Catharine. 1989. *Toward a Feminist Theory of the State.* Cambridge, Mass.: Harvard University Press.

MacKinnon, Catharine. 2006. *Are Women Human? And Other International Dialogues.* Cambridge, Mass.: Belknap Press, 2006.

Madriz, Esther. 1997. "Images of Criminals and Victims: A Study on Women's Fear and Social Control." *Gender and Society* 11 (3): 342–56.

Maldonado-Torres, Nelson. 2007 "On the Coloniality of Being: Contributions to the Development of a Concept." *Cultural Studies* 21 (2–3): 240–70.

Mann, Bonnie. 2006. *Women's Liberation and the Sublime: Feminism, Postmodernism, Environment.* Oxford: Oxford University Press.

Mann, Bonnie. 2008. "Beauvoir and the Question of a Woman's Point of View." *Philosophy Today* 52 (2): 136–49.

Mann, Bonnie. 2012. "Creepers, Flirts, Heroes, and Allies: Four Theses on Men and Sexual Harassment." *APA Newsletter on Feminism and Philosophy* 11 (2): 24–31.

Mann, Bonnie. 2014. *Sovereign Masculinity: Gender Lessons from the War on Terror.* Oxford: Oxford University Press.

Mann, Bonnie. 2017. "Beauvoir against Objectivism: The Operation of the Norm in Beauvoir and Butler." In *On Ne Naît Pas Femme: On Le Devient: The Life of a Sentence*, edited by Bonnie Mann and Martina Ferrari, 37–54. Oxford: Oxford University Press.

Manne, Kate. 2018. *Down Girl: The Logic of Misogyny.* Oxford: Oxford University Press.

Marcus, Sharon. 1992. "Fighting Bodies, Fighting Words: A Theory and Politics of Rape Prevention." In *Feminists Theorize the Political*, edited by Judith Butler and Joan Scott, 385–403. New York: Routledge.

McCaughey, Martha. 1997. *Real Knockouts: The Physical Feminism of Women's Self-Defense.* New York: New York University Press.

McWeeny, Jennifer. 2017. "*The Second Sex* of Consciousness: A New Temporality and Ontology for Beauvoir's 'Becoming a Woman.'" In *On Ne Naît Pas Femme: On Le Devient: The Life of a Sentence*, edited by Bonnie Mann and Martina Ferrari, 231–74. Oxford: Oxford University Press.

McWhorter, Ladelle. 2009. *Racism and Sexual Oppression in Anglo-America.* Indianapolis: Indiana University Press.

Merleau-Ponty, Maurice. 1968. *The Visible and the Invisible.* Translated by Alphonso Lingis. Evanston, Ill.: Northwestern University Press.

Merleau-Ponty, Maurice. 1993. "Eye and Mind." In *The Merleau-Ponty Aesthetics Reader*, edited by Ted Toadvine and Leonard Lawlor, translated by Galen A. Johnson, 351–78. Evanston, Ill.: Northwestern University Press.

Merleau-Ponty, Maurice. 2012. *Phenomenology of Perception.* Translated by Donald A. Landes. London: Routledge.

Mignolo, Walter. 2002. "The Geopolitics of Knowledge and the Colonial Difference." *South Atlantic Quarterly* 101 (1): 57–96.

Mignolo, Walter. 2011. *The Darker Side of Western Modernity: Global Futures, Decolonial Options.* Durham, N.C.: Duke University Press.

Miller, Elaine. 2012. "Saving Time: Temporality, Recurrence, and Transcendence in Beauvoir's Nietzschean Cycles." In *Beauvoir and Western Thought from Plato to Butler*, edited by Shannon Mussett and William Wilkerson, 103–24. New York: State University of New York Press.

Miller, Sarah Clark. 2009. "Moral Injury and Relational Harm: Analyzing Rape in Darfur." *Journal of Social Philosophy* 40 (4): 504–23.

Mogul, Joey, Andrea Ritchie, and Kay Whitlock. 2011. *Queer (In)justice: The Criminalization of LGBT People in the United States.* Boston: Beacon Press.

Moi, Toril. 2001. *What Is a Woman? And Other Essays.* Oxford: Oxford University Press.

Moi, Toril. 2008. *Simone de Beauvoir: The Making of an Intellectual Woman.* 2nd ed. Oxford: Oxford University Press.

Murphy, Ann. 2012. *Violence and the Philosophical Imaginary.* Albany: State University of New York Press.

Oksala, Johanna. 2006. "A Phenomenology of Gender." *Continental Philosophy Review* 39 (3): 229–44.

Oliver, Kelly. 2016. *Hunting Girls: Sexual Violence from The Hunger Games to Campus Rape.* New York: Columbia University Press.

Ortega, Mariana. 2016. *In-Between: Latina Feminist Phenomenology, Multiplicity, and the Self.* Albany: State University of New York Press.

Oyĕwùmì, Oyèrónké. 1997. *The Invention of Women: Making an African Sense of Western Gender Discourses.* Minneapolis: University of Minnesota Press.

Pascoe, C. J. 2007. *Dude You're a Fag: Masculinity and Sexuality in High School.* Berkeley: University of California Press.

Phillips, Lynn M. 2000. *Flirting with Danger: Young Women's Reflections on Sexuality and Domination.* New York: New York University Press.

Quijano, Aníbal. 2000a. "Colonialidad del Poder y Clasificacion Social." *Journal of World-Systems Research* 11 (2): 342–86.

Quijano, Aníbal. 2000b. "Coloniality of Power, Eurocentrism, and Latin America." *Nepantla: Views from the South* 1 (3): 533–80.

Rhodan, Maya. 2016. "Donald Trump Raises Eyebrows with 'Bad Hombres' Line." *Time*, October 20, 2016. http://time.com/.

Rich, Adrienne. 1980. "Compulsory Heterosexuality and Lesbian Existence." *Signs* 5 (4): 631–60.

Ritchie, Andrea. 2017. *Invisible No More: Police Violence against Black Women and Women of Color.* Boston: Beacon Press.

Root, Maria. 1992. "Reconstructing the Impact of Trauma on Personality." In *Personality and Psychopathology: Feminist Reappraisals*, edited by Laura Brown and Mary Ballou, 229–65. New York: Guilford Press.

Russonello, Giovanni. 2018. "Read Oprah Winfrey's Golden Globes Speech." *New York Times*, January 7, 2018. https://www.nytimes.com/.

Ryan, Kathryn. 2011. "The Relationship between Rape Myths and Sexual Scripts: The Social Construction of Rape." *Sex Roles* 65 (11–12): 774–82.

Scarth, Frederika. 2004. *The Other Within: Ethics, Politics, and the Body in Simone de Beauvoir.* Lanham, Md.: Rowman & Littlefield.

Schank, Roger, and Robert Abelson. 1977. *Scripts, Plans, Goals, and Understanding: An Inquiry into Human Knowledge Structures.* London: Psychology Press.

Schües, Christina, Dorothea Olkowski, and Helen Fielding, eds. 2011. *Time in Feminist Phenomenology.* Bloomington: Indiana University Press.

Sedgwick, Eve Kosofsky. 1993. "Queer Performativity: Henry James's *The Art of the Novel.*" *GLQ: A Journal of Gay and Lesbian Studies* 1 (1): 1–16.

Sheffield, Carole. 1987. "Sexual Terrorism." In *Gender Violence: Interdisciplinary Perspectives,* edited by Laura O'Toole, Jessica Schiffman, and Margie L. Kiter Edwards, 110–28. New York: New York University Press.

Simms, Eva-Maria, and Beata Stawarska. 2014. "Introduction: Concepts and Methods in Interdisciplinary Feminist Phenomenology." *Janus Head* 13 (1): 6–16.

Simons, Margaret. 1999. *Beauvoir and "The Second Sex": Feminism, Race, and the Origins of Existentialism.* Lanham, Md.: Rowman & Littlefield.

Smith, Andrea. 2005. *Conquest: Sexual Violence and American Genocide.* Cambridge, Mass.: South End Press.

Spade, Dean. 2003. "Resisting Medicine, Re/modeling Gender." *Berkeley Women's Law Journal* 18 (1): 15–37.

Spelman, Elizabeth. 1988. *The Inessential Woman: Problems of Exclusion in Feminist Thought.* Boston: Beacon Press.

Spivak, Gayatri. 1995. "Ghostwriting." *Diacritics* 25 (2): 65–84.

Stanley, Eric, Nat Smith, and CeCe McDonald, eds. 2015. *Captive Genders: Trans Embodiment and the Prison Industrial Complex.* 2nd ed. Edinburgh: A. K. Press.

Stoller, Silvia. 2009. "Phenomenology and the Poststructural Critique of Experience." *International Journal of Philosophical Studies* 17 (5): 707–37.

Stoller, Silvia. 2010. "Expressivity and Performativity: Merleau-Ponty and Butler." *Continental Philosophy Review* 43 (1): 97–110.

Stoller, Silvia. 2011. "Gender and Anonymous Temporality." In *Time in Feminist Phenomenology,* edited by Christina Schües, Dorothea Olkowski, and Helen A. Fielding, 79–90. Bloomington: Indiana University Press.

Stoller, Silvia. 2014. "The Indeterminable Gender: Ethics in Feminist Phenomenology and Poststructuralist Feminism." *Janus Head* 13 (1): 17–34.

Sullivan, Shannon. 2001. *Living Across and Through Skins: Transactional Bodies, Pragmatism, and Feminism.* Indianapolis: Indiana University Press.

Szymanski, Dawn M., and Kimberly F. Balsam. 2011. "Insidious Trauma: Examining the Relationship between Heterosexism and Lesbians' PTSD Symptoms." *Traumatology* 17 (2): 4–13.

Tidd, Ursula. 1999. *Simone de Beauvoir, Gender, and Testimony*. Cambridge: Cambridge University Press.

Tidd, Ursula. 2011. "For the Time Being: Simone de Beauvoir's Representation of Temporality." In *The Existential Phenomenology of Simone de Beauvoir*, edited by Wendy O'Brien and Lester Embree, 107–26. Dordrecht: Kluwer Academic.

U.S. Attorney's Office. 2015. "Full Dylan Roof Confession." *New York Times*, December 10, 2016. https://www.nytimes.com/.

U.S. Bureau of Justice; Office of Justice Programs. 2013. *Female Victims of Sexual Violence, 1994–2010*. March 31, 2013. https://www.bjs.gov/content/pub/pdf/fvsv 9410.pdf.

Valentine, Gill. 1989. "The Geography of Women's Fear." *Area* 21 (4): 385–90.

Valentine, Gill. 1992. "Images of Danger: Women's Sources of Information about the Spatial Distribution of Male Violence." *Area* 24 (1): 22–29.

Vallega, Alejandro. 2014. *Latin American Philosophy from Identity to Radical Exteriority*. Indianapolis: Indiana University Press.

van der Kolk, Bessel. 2015. *The Body Keeps the Score: Brain, Mind, and Body in the Healing of Trauma*. New York: Penguin.

Veltman, Andrea. 2006. "Transcendence and Immanence in the Ethics of Simone de Beauvoir." In *The Philosophy of Simone de Beauvoir*, edited by Margaret Simons, 113–31. Bloomington: Indiana University Press.

Vera-Grey, Fiona. 2017. *Men's Intrusion, Women's Embodiment: A Critical Analysis of Street Harassment*. New York: Routledge.

Washington Post. 2015. "Full Text: Donald Trump Announces a Presidential Bid." June 16, 2015. https://www.washingtonpost.com/.

Waters, Anne. 2004. "Language Matters: Nondiscreet Nonbinary Dualism." In *American Indian Thought: Philosophical Essays*, edited by Anne Waters, 97–115. Malden, Mass.: Blackwell.

Wells, Ida B. 1892. "Southern Horrors: Lynch Law in All Its Phases." Project Gutenberg. https://www.gutenberg.org/.

Wells, Ida B. 1895. "The Red Record." Project Gutenberg. https://www.gutenberg .org/.

West, Candace, and Don Zimmerman. 1987. "Doing Gender." *Gender and Society* 1 (2): 125–51.

Westbrook, Laurel, and Kristen Schilt. 2015. "Penis Panics: Biological Maleness, Social Masculinity, and the Matrix of Perceived Sexual Threat." In *Exploring Masculinities: Identity, Inequality, Continuity, and Change*, edited by C. J. Pascoe and Tristan Bridges. 382–93. Oxford: Oxford University Press.

Workman, Karen, and Andrea Kannapell. 2015. "The Charleston Shooting: What Happened." *New York Times*, June 18, 2015. https://www.nytimes.com/.

Yancy, George. 2008. *Black Bodies, White Gazes: The Continuing Significance of Race*. Lanham, Md.: Rowman & Littlefield.

Yavorsky, Jill E., and Liana Sayer. 2013. "'Doing Fear': The Influence of Hetero-femininity on (Trans)women's Fears of Victimization." *Sociological Quarterly* 54 (4): 511–33.

Young, Iris Marion. 1980. "Throwing Like a Girl: A Phenomenology of Feminine Body Comportment Motility and Spatiality." *Human Studies* 3 (2): 137–56.

Young, Iris Marion. 2005. *On Female Body Experience: "Throwing Like a Girl" and Other Essays.* Oxford: Oxford University Press.

Index

MEGAN BURKE is assistant professor of philosophy at Sonoma State University in California.

Made in the USA
Middletown, DE
14 February 2020